Boost Spelling Skills 2

Strategies, Tips and Practice
Activities to Develop and
Improve Pupils'
Word Pattern Recognition
in Lower KS2

Judy Arden

Judy Arden (Thornby) is an experienced former primary teacher and specialist in learning support. She has taught pupils with a range of abilities for over 25 years, gaining a Diploma in Specific Learning Difficulties in 1999. Being enthusiastic about promoting literacy skills, she has written the '*Boost Spelling Skills*' series for KS1 and KS2, and older pupils who struggle with spelling. She has also written the '*Boost Creative Writing Skills*' series.

Published by Brilliant Publications Limited
Unit 10
Sparrow Hall Farm
Edlesborough
Dunstable
Bedfordshire
LU6 2ES, UK

www.brilliantpublications.co.uk

Brilliant Publications is a registered trademark.

Written by Judy Arden
Illustrations: Brilliant Publications Limited
Cover: Molly Sage
© Brilliant Publications Limited 2022

Printed ISBN: 978-0-85747-985-3
PDF ISBN: 978-0-85747-987-7
First printed and published in the UK in 2023
10 9 8 7 6 5 4 3 2 1

The right of Judy Arden to be identified as the author of this work has been asserted by her in accordance with the Copyright, Designs and Patents Act 1988.

All rights reserved. Apart from any use permitted under UK copyright law, no part of this publication may be reproduced or transmitted in any form or by any means, electronic or mechanical, including photocopying and recording, or held within any information storage and retrieval system, without permission in writing from the publishers or under licence from the Copyright Licensing Agency Limited. Further details of such licenses (for reprographic reproduction) may be obtained from the Copyright Licensing Agency Limited, 5th Floor, Shackleton House, 4 Battle Bridge Lane, London SE1 2HX (https://cla.co.uk)

Contents

Introduction
About the Book 6–7

Spelling Strategies
Different Spelling Strategies..8–10
Look, Say, Cover, Write, Check, Pro Forma...11–13
Memory Joggers...14–18
Compound Words: *Worksheets*..19–20
Split Words into Syllables – Rules of Syllabification: *Teacher's Tips*.......................................21
Split Words into Syllables – Rules of Syllabification: *Worksheet*..22
Link Words with the Same Letter Pattern..23–24

Keywords
Keywords 1 25
Keywords 2 26

Suffixes
Suffixes 27–28
'-ic' '-ive' Words: *Spelling Sheet*..29
'-ic', '-ive' Words: *Reading Text*..30
'-ic', '-ive' Words: *Worksheets*...31–32
'-ous' '-ious' Words: *Spelling Sheet*..33
'-ous' '-ious' Words: *Reading Text*...34
'-ous' '-ious' Words: *Worksheets*...35–36
'-ly', '-ally' Words: *Spelling Sheet*...37
'-ly', '-ally' Words: *Reading Text*...38
'-ly', '-ally' Words: *Worksheets*..39–40
'-sure' '-ture' Words: *Spelling Sheet*...41
'-sure' '-ture' Words: *Reading Text*..42
'-sure' '-ture' Words: *Worksheet*..43
'-tian', '-sion', '-cian' Words: *Spelling Sheet*...44
'-tian', '-sion', '-cian' Words: *Reading Text*..45
'-tian', '-sion', '-cian' Words: *Worksheets*..46–47
'-ation' Words: *Spellsheet*...48
'-ation' Words: *Worksheet*..49
Syllable Splitting Rules: *Teacher's Tips*..50
Syllable Splits: *Worksheets*..51–52

Dictation Exercises
Suffixes: *Teacher Tips* 53–55

Suffix Spelling Rules
Double Letter Rule 56
'y' Rule 56
'e' Rule 56
Double Letter Rule: *Worksheet* 57
'e' Rule: *Worksheets* 58–59
'y' Rule: *Worksheets* 60–61

Dictation Exercises
Sufix Spelling Rules: *Teacher's Tips* 62

Functions of Suffixes
Making Comparatives: Adding Vowel Suffixes '-er' and '-est': *Teacher's Tips* 63
Making Comparatives: *Worksheets* 64–65
Making Plurals: Adding '-s' or '-es': *Teacher's Tips* 66
Making Plurals 1: *Worksheet* 67
Making Plurals 2: *Worksheet* 68
Making Plurals 3: *Worksheet* 69
Making Plurals 4: *Worksheet* 70
Making Plurals 5: *Worksheet* 71
Changing Tense: Adding '-ed' or '-ing': *Worksheets* 72–73
Changing Parts of Speech: Nouns into Adjectives: *Worksheet* 74
Changing Parts of Speech: Verbs and Adjectives into Nouns: *Worksheet* 75
Changing Parts of Speech: Adjectives and Nouns into Verbs: *Worksheet* 76

Prefixes
'ex-', 'dis-' Words: *Spelling Sheet* 77
'ex-' Words: *Reading Text* 78
'dis-' Words: *Reading Text* 79
'ex-', 'dis-' Words: *Worksheets* 80–81
'pro-', 're-' Words: *Spelling Sheet* 82
'pro-' Words: *Reading Text* 83
're-' Words: *Reading Text* 84
'pro-', 're-' Words: *Worksheets* 85–86
'pre-', 'sub-', 'super-', ' tele-' Words: *Worksheet* 87
'pre-', 'sub-', 'super-', ' tele-' Words: *Reading Text* 88

'pre-', 'sub-', 'super-', ' tele-' Words: *Worksheets* 89–90
Derivations of Prefix 'in' 91–93
Prefix Syllable Splits: *Worksheets* 94–95

Dictation Exercises
Prefixes: *Teacher's Tips* 96

Root Words
Root Words: *Worksheet* 97
Sort the Root: *Worksheet* 98
Word Origins: *Teacher's Tips* 99
Root Word Origins: 'ch' saying /k/ or 'ch' saying /sh/ Words: *Spelling Sheet* 100
Root Word Origins: 'ch' saying /k/ or 'ch' saying /sh/ Words: *Reading Text* 101
Root Word Origins: 'ch' saying /k/ or 'ch' saying /sh/ Words: *Worksheet* 102
Root Origins Game: Match Words With Their Meanings 103–104

Homophones
Homophones Lists or Game 105–110
Homophones: *Worksheets* 111–112
Homophones 'to', 'two','too': *Worksheet* 113
Homophones 'there', 'their', 'they're': *Worksheet* 114
Near Homophones, 'accept/except': *Worksheet* 115
Near Homophones, 'affect/effect': *Worksheet* 116
Homophone Sound Pairs Game: *Snap Cards* 117–120

Dictation Exercises
Homophones: *Teacher's Tips* 121

Silent Letters
Silent Letters: *Reading Text* 122
Silent Letters: *Worksheet* 123
Silent Letters: Card Game 124–127

Dictation Exercises
Silent Letters: *Teacher's Tips* 128

Appendix 1: Glossary 129–130
Appendix 2: Irregular Verbs Past Tense 131
Photo / Illustration Credits 132

Introduction

About the Book

Boost Spelling Skills 2 is designed for use at lower KS2 level and can also be used by older pupils who find spelling challenging. The book follows DFES National literacy guidelines for spelling for the 7–9 years age group and is divided into nine sections:

1. Spelling Strategies
2. Keywords
3. Suffixes
4. Suffix Spelling Rules
5. Functions of Suffixes
6. Prefixes
7. Root words
8. Homophones
9. Silent Letters

Boost Spelling Skills 2 extends the various strategies taught in Key Stage 1 (KS1) to help pupils improve their spelling. These strategies include using memory joggers and looking for smaller words within longer ones – to help the pupil spell the tricky part of a word. Identifying the root or base word and recognising the prefix and suffix is a useful strategy as is splitting a longer difficult word into easier bite size syllables. A 'Look, Say, Cover, Write, Check' (LSCWC) pro forma is included as this is a tried and trusted strategy to promote good spelling skills, by using visual auditory and kinaesthetic cues in a multisensory approach.

A focus of the book is to investigate prefixes, roots or base words and suffixes which are the building blocks of words. It explores how suffixes and prefixes can modify the meaning and spelling of the word. Adding a suffix can change a word into an adjective, noun or adverb as well as changing the tense of a word.

Many words have their origins in Latin or Greek. It is helpful to identify the meaning of some word roots as it extends vocabulary and provides support for spelling. For example the root *'annus'* comes from the Latin word meaning 'year' and can be noticed in words such as *'annual'*, *'anniversary'* and *'annuity'* Research shows that pupils who have a good understanding of word structures have better spelling and reading comprehension skills.

There is emphasis on the main spelling rules that apply when adding suffixes which include the **double consonant** rule, 'e' and 'y' rules. Developing knowledge of these rules will give an understanding of how the spelling of the base word can change when adding a suffix, although there are always some exceptions to these rules.

Introduction

The book contains lists of spellings, reading activities and worksheets which provide reinforcement to the specific letter pattern, suffix/prefix ending or spelling rule covered. In the reading passages, the pupil is asked to highlight the target letter pattern whilst reading. Targeted dictation exercises and spelling games provide further opportunity for consolidation.

Sections on homophones and silent letters build on the work covered at KS1 level. It is important to have awareness of silent letters, as they are prominent in the English language and affect more than half the letters of the alphabet.

Spelling Strategies

hip/po/pot/am/us

There are various helpful spelling strategies in which you can boost spelling:

Invent a mnemonic that jogs the memory for spelling trickier words.

For example: **build**

<u>B</u>asically, <u>U</u> and <u>I</u> <u>L</u>ove <u>D</u>ogs

Become a *Word Detective*:
Look for smaller words inside longer words.

For example:

vegetable = get, table, able

business = bus, sin, in

Notice compound words.

For example:

heavyweight: heavy / weight

somewhere: some / where

knowledge: know / ledge

Boost Spelling Skills 2

©Brilliant Publications Limited

Spelling Strategies

hip/po/pot/am/us

Split the words into syllables – bite size pieces are easier to recall.

For example: hippopotamus

hip/po/pot/am/us

Link words with the same letter sequence.

For example:

could   would   should

Take an irregularly spelt word and say it wrongly – pronounce it exactly how it looks.

For example:

Wed-nes-day   bus-in-ess

Use a 'Look, Say, Cover, Write, Check' approach when learning new spellings.

Spelling Strategies

hip/po/pot/am/us

Spot the prefix and the suffix to identify the root/base word.

For example: **disappointment**

dis – appoint – ment

Link words with the same root.

For example: <u>act</u>

<u>act</u>or : <u>act</u>ion : extr<u>act</u>

cont<u>act</u> : re<u>act</u>ion

Spelling Strategies

hip/po/pot/am/us

Look, Say, Cover, Write, Check

LOOK 	at the word carefully. Can you see a smaller word in it? Is there a tricky bit? Notice if there is a prefix or suffix.
SAY 	the word out loud. How many syllables does it have?
COVER 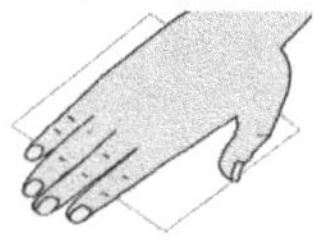	the word up when you think you have remembered it.
WRITE 	the word down without looking.
CHECK 	Have you written the word correctly? Repeat again five times.

Guidelines

Look at the word and make a picture of it in your head. Say the word out loud then cover it up before writing it down. Let the movement of the pen help the memory of the shape of the word. Finally check if it has been spelt correctly. Correct if needed and write again. This is an effective way of imprinting the word to memory as it uses a multisensory approach. Multisensory learning involves visual, auditory and kinaesthetic tactile prompts and is a helpful strategy for all pupils. A 'Look, Say, Cover, Write, Check' pro forma is on the next pages (12–13).

©Brilliant Publications Limited

Spelling Strategies

Look, Say, Cover, Write, Check

hip/po/pot/am/us

Look at the word. Say the word.	Cover the word. Write out the word.	check									

Boost Spelling Skills 2

Spelling Strategies

Look, Say, Cover, Write, Check

hip/po/pot/am/us

Word	1st Try	2nd Try	3rd Try

Spelling Strategies

Memory Joggers

hip/po/pot/am/us

Mnemonics or memory joggers can help spell trickier words. They are often used as a reminder for commonly used key words which are irregularly spelt. A memory jogger can be used to remember the whole word or just the tricky part.

Try making up your own!

BEAUTIFUL	**E**lephants **A**nd **U**nicorns are b**eau**tiful.
BELIEVE	I beli**eve** in **EVE**.
BUILD	**B**asically, **U** and **I** **L**ove **D**ogs.
FAVOURITE	**OUR** fav**our**ite colour is red.
FRUIT	**U** and **I** eat fruit.
HEARD	I h**ear**d with my **EAR**.
HEIGHT	**HE** has **He**ight.
ISLAND	There **IS LAND** on the **island**.
LAUGH	**L**augh **a**nd **U** **g**et **h**appy.
PIECE	Can I have a **pie**ce of **PIE**?
SEPARATE	There is **A RAT** in sep**a**r**at**e.
SPECIAL	*Special* **P**eople **E**at **C**ake **I**n **A** **L**ibrary.
THOUGHT	(I **thought**) **O**ld **U**ncle **G**ary **H**ated **T**arantulas.
YOUNG	**YOU** are **you**ng.

Boost Spelling Skills 2

Memory Joggers

beautiful

<u>E</u>lephants <u>a</u>nd <u>U</u>nicorns are b<u>eau</u>tiful!

believe

I beli<u>eve</u> in <u>Eve</u>

build

<u>B</u>asically,
<u>U</u> and <u>I</u>
<u>L</u>ove <u>D</u>ogs

Memory Joggers

favourite

<u>O</u>ur fav<u>ou</u>rite colour is red.

fruit

<u>U</u> and <u>I</u> eat fruit

heard

I h<u>ear</u>d with my <u>ear</u>.

Memory Joggers

height

<u>He</u>
has <u>hei</u>ght

island

There <u>is</u> <u>land</u> on that <u>island</u>

laugh

<u>L</u>augh <u>a</u>nd <u>U</u> get <u>h</u>appy

Memory Joggers

thought

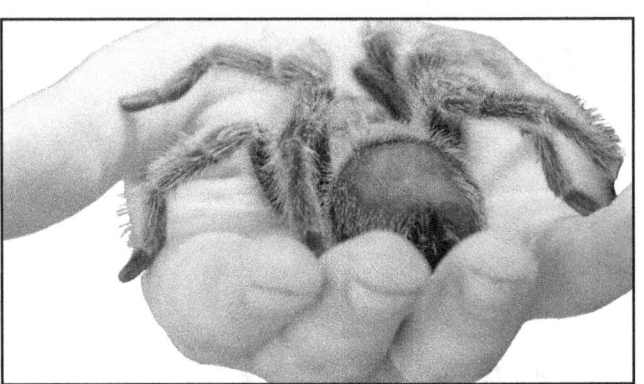

I thought
<u>O</u>ld <u>U</u>ncle <u>G</u>ary
<u>H</u>ated <u>T</u>arantulas!

young

<u>You</u> are <u>you</u>ng

piece

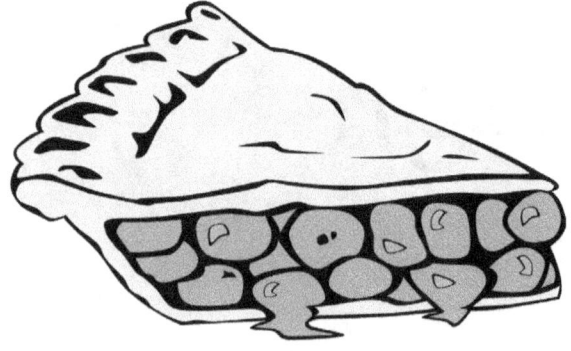

Can I have a p<u>ie</u>ce of p<u>ie</u>?

Spelling Strategies

hip/po/pot/am/us

Compound Words

Compound words are two or three whole words that can be combined to make one word.

They are usually nouns. For example:

break + fast = breakfast

Put the two smaller words together to form a new word.

1. news + paper = _____

2. earth + quake = _____

3. black + bird = _____

4. paint + brush = _____

5. farm + yard = _____

6. dust + bin = _____

7. fair + ground = _____

Boost Spelling Skills 2

Spelling Strategies

Compound Words

hip/po/pot/am/us

Join two words together (one word from each column) to make a new word.

foot	1. _____	room
good	2. _____	end
cup	3. _____	stairs
week	4. _____	night
wheel	5. _____	ball
grass	6. _____	shine
down	7. _____	cake
cloak	8. _____	chair
play	9. _____	ground
sun	10. _____	hopper

Create a list of compound words from the base word.

1. any	anyone	anybody	anywhere	anything
2. no				
3. some				
4. every				

Boost Spelling Skills 2

©Brilliant Publications Limited

Spelling Strategies

Split Words into Syllables

hip/po/pot/am/us

Rules of Syllabification

Compound word syllable
Split between the two smaller words inside it.
For example: sauce/pan   news/paper   earth/worm

Open syllable
If a single consonant comes between two vowels – split before the consonant to keep vowel long (V/C/V)
For example: fre/quent   stu/dent   fa/mous

Closed syllable
If a single consonant comes between two vowels – split after the consonant to keep the vowel short (V/C/V)
For example: plan/et   cam/el   im/ag/ine

Short vowel sound + two consonants (VC/CV)
Split between the two consonants
For example: ap/pear   ag/gres/sive

If more than two consonants split **keep** blends together
For example: mon/ster   ap/prove

Consonant + 'le' syllable
If a word ends in a consonant + le, split before the consonant. If there are two consonants + le split in between the consonants.
For example: ta/ble   crum/ple   daz/zle

'r' combination
- Split after ur, ar, ir
For example : cur/tain   tar/get   cir/cus

REMEMBER
* Split the prefixes and suffixes from the base or root word.
  For example :   dis/appoint/ment   pro/tect/ed

* Every syllable has at least one vowel or part time vowel 'y'.

Boost Spelling Skills 2

©Brilliant Publications Limited

hip/po/pot/am/us

Spelling Strategies

Split Words into Syllables
Rules of Syllabification

Read the words below and split into syllables.

Tip: Watch out for the open syllable as in 'spi / der' ending in a long vowel and identify the suffix in each word

adventure	ad/ven/ture
disinfectant	
probably	
alternative	
uninterested	
generosity	
dangerous	
population	
university	
frequently	
indecisive	
examination	
consider	
characteristic	
independence	
accident	
confidential	

Boost Spelling Skills 2

Spelling Strategies

Link Words With Same Letter Pattern

hip/po/pot/am/us

Using the patterns from words you know how to spell is another strategy which can be useful when breaking down unknown words.

Try these.

h
c
sn
th
scr
w

atch

_____
_____
_____
_____
_____
_____

w
h
pl
dr
knowl

edge

_____
_____
_____
_____
_____

m
j
cr
gr
st

umble

_____
_____
_____
_____
_____

Boost Spelling Skills 2

Spelling Strategies

Link Words With Same Letter Pattern

Draw lines to match up the rhyming words and then write them down below.

bought
eight
city
strength
niece
should

length
piece
thought
could
weight
pity

1. _____   _____
2. _____   _____
3. _____   _____
4. _____   _____
5. _____   _____
6. _____   _____

Keywords

Keywords 1

after	again	any	across	asked
bath	beautiful	because	before	behind
break	busy	called	children	Christmas
class	climb	clothes	cold	coming
could	cousin	cried	does	door
everybody	eye	fast	father	find
floor	friend	giant	going	grass
great	half	hold	hour	improve
jumped	kind	know	last	little
laugh	looked	magic	many	money
move	next	night	once	only
our	parents	pass	past	people
plant	please	poor	pretty	put
pulled	quiet	really	said	saw
school	should	some	steak	stopped
suddenly	sugar	sure	their	they're
thought	through	told	Tuesday	use
very	walk	want	was	water
were	where	which	who	whole
wild	work	world	would	your

Commonly used irregularly spelt words which can be misspelt at the start of Year 3. (Taken from 'National Literacy Strategy Appendix 1 Year 2 Exception Words' and 'Letters and Sounds High Frequency Spelt Words' published by DFE).

Keywords

Keywords 2

accident (ally)	actual (ly)	address	answer	appear
arrive	believe	bicycle	breath	breathe
build	busy/business	calendar	caught	centre
century	certain	circle	complete	consider
continue	decide	describe	different	difficult
disappear	early	earth	eight/eighty	enough
exercise	experience	experiment	extreme	famous
favourite	February	forward (s)	fruit	grammar
group	guard	guide	heard	heart
height	history	imagine	increase	important
interest	island	knowledge	learn	length
library	material	medicine	mention	minute
natural	naughty	notice	occasion (ally)	often
opposite	ordinary	particular	peculiar	perhaps
popular	position	possess (ion)	possible	potatoes
pressure	probably	promise	purpose	quarter
question	recent	regular	reign	remember
sentence	separate	special	straight	strange
strength	suppose	surprise	therefore	though/although
thought	through	various	weight	woman/women

Words that pupils are expected to spell by age 9.

Department for Education, 2013, The National Curriculum in England.
Re-used under the terms of the Open Government Licence.

Boost Spelling Skills 2

Suffixes

Suffixes

creative

A suffix is a letter or a group of letters which is added to the end of a word to form a new word.

-ic -ive	'-ive' or '-ic' turns nouns and verbs into adjectives. Drop the final 'e' or 'y' and add the vowel suffixes.	allergy – allergic create – creative
-ous	If the word is an adjective use '-ous' NB: If the word is a noun use '-us'. If the word ends '-our', change to '-or' before adding '-ous'. If a word ends in '-ge', keep the 'e'	anxious poisonous cactus, genius, octopus glam<u>ou</u>r – glam<u>o</u>rous coura<u>ge</u> – coura<u>ge</u>ous outra<u>ge</u> – outra<u>ge</u>ous

Sometimes the root word is obvious and the usual rules apply for adding suffixes beginning with vowel letters. Sometimes there is no obvious root word.

-ed	Add '-ed' to verbs to show past tense.	clap – clapped look – looked
-er	Add '-er' to verbs – to show person doing action.	run – runner dive – diver
	Add '-er' to adjectives to create a comparative.	happy – happier ugly – uglier
-est	Add '-est' to adjectives to create a superlative.	short – shortest sunny – sunniest
-es	Add '-es' to nouns to show plural.	foxes – churches
	Add '-es' to verbs to show present tense.	crouch – crouches relax – relaxes
-ing	Add '-ing' to verbs to show progressive form.	shop – shopping hope – hoping

Teacher's Tips (repeated down right margin)

Boost Spelling Skills 2

©Brilliant Publications Limited

Suffixes

Suffix	Guidlines	Examples
-ly	Adding suffix '**-ly**' to an adjective turns the word into an adverb.	quiet – quietly
	If the root word ends in <u>consonant + y</u> change '**y**' to '**i**' before adding '**-ly**'.	happy – happily
	If the root word ends in '**ic**', just add '**-ally**'.	frantic – frantically

Suffix	Guidlines	Examples
-sure	Use with words having /zur/ sound ending.	measure, treasure
-ture	Often used with words having /chur/ sound ending.	creature, furniture

Suffix	Guidlines	Examples
-tion	Most common with /shun/ sound endings, use suffix '**ation**' added to verbs to form nouns.	prepare – preparation visualize – visualisation
-sion	If the root word ends in '**d/de**' or '**-se**', '**-sion**' is usually used.	expand – expansion supervise – supervision
-cian	Use '**-cian**' for people's jobs.	politician musician magician

See also sections on Functions of Suffixes (page 63–76) and Suffix Spelling Rules (pages 56–61).

Boost Spelling Skills 2

Suffixes

'-ic', '-ive' Words

Can you read and spell these words?

creative

Set A		Set B	
'-ic' words	'-ive' words	'-ic' words	'-ive' words
music	active	chaotic	detective
comic	forgive	volcanic	talkative
picnic	captive	allergic	protective
traffic	creative	epidemic	adjective
heroic	positive	mechanic	aggressive
organic	massive	automatic	attractive
electric	relative	scientific	imaginative
athletic	inactive	energetic	decorative
gigantic	negative	optimistic	exclusive
fantastic	expensive	sympathetic	destructive

Guidance:

'-**ic**' is often used to form <u>adjectives</u> from <u>nouns</u>, for example: metal = metallic, poet = poetic.

'-**ive**' words are often adjectives.

Can you make sentences using some of the words from the table?

1. _____
2. _____
3. _____
4. _____
5. _____

Boost Spelling Skills 2

Suffixes

'-ic', '-ive' Words

creative

Read and highlight the '-ic' and '-ive' words.

My relative, Uncle Cedric, is always energetic just before Christmas. He always likes to make the outside of his house and garden attractive with lots of decorative Christmassy things. Over time he has gathered all sorts of Christmas decorations, which he stores in his attic. However, every year Uncle Cedric makes something else imaginative and inventive! This year he built a sledge and a Santa Claus which he cleverly illuminated in a light display in his front garden. Then he put up the fantastic decorations he already had from previous years. After that he strung up lots of festive lights which twinkled on his trees and bushes. It took him several days to complete but his display was pure magic and looked so impressive once he had finished. Everybody in his neighbourhood is always appreciative of all his hard work and his house always attracts crowds of visitors around Christmas time. Sometimes, so many cars come down his road to see the decorations on his house that they cause a mini traffic jam! I am just wondering what creative ideas my Uncle Cedric will think of for next year!

Find and write down six different words from the passage that end in '-ic'.

1. _____   2. _____
3. _____   4. _____
5. _____   6. _____

Split these words into syllables.

impressive	im/press/ive
decorative	
imaginative	
optimistic	

Suffixes

'-ic', '-ive' Words

creative

| comic | traffic | relative | allergic | gigantic |
| adjective | expensive | protective | heroic | topic |

Choose the correct word from the box above to complete the sentences.

1. I like to read a _____ at bedtime.
2. Uncle Tom and Aunty Jill are my _____ s.
3. Jack climbed up the _____ beanstalk in the story.
4. That bike is too _____ so you must choose a cheaper one.
5. The knight was _____ to fight the dragon.
6. Lara had an _____ reaction to the cat and began sneezing.
7. All the cars on the road have caused a huge _____ jam.
8. An _____ is a word that describes a noun in a sentence.
9. The nurse wore _____ clothing so she did not catch the virus.
10. Jack is enjoying the _____ about the Romans.

Boost Spelling Skills 2
©Brilliant Publications Limited

Suffixes

'-ic', '-ive' Words

creat<u>ive</u>

Draw lines to match the word to its meaning.

disruptive		a fast spreading disease
heroic		causing trouble
repulsive		something which is disgusting
adjective		pleasant to look at
epidemic		being very brave
attractive		a describing word

Add 'ic' to form adjectives from these nouns.

1. hero   <u>heroic</u>
2. magnet _____
3. artist _____
4. poet _____
5. idiot _____
6. alcohol _____
7. diplomat _____
8. telegraph _____

Suffixes

'-ous', '-ious' Words

creative

Can you read and spell these words?

Set A		Set B	
'-ous' words	'-ious' words	'-ous' words	'-ious' words
famous	various	glamorous	anxious
nervous	serious	outrageous	cautious
enormous	obvious	marvellous	delicious
tremendous	curious	adventurous	luxurious
dangerous	precious	anonymous	nutritious
numerous	spacious	carnivorous	mysterious
poisonous	envious	courageous	suspicious
disastrous	furious	ridiculous	scrumptious
jealous	previous	mischievous	unconscious
hazardous	infectious	advantageous	superstitious

Guidance:
If the word is an adjective use **'-ous'**.
'-our' is changed to **'-or'** before **'-ous'** is added, glamour – glam<u>o</u>rous.
For words ending **'-ge'**, keep the **'e'** and add **'-ous'**, coura<u>ge</u>ous, outra<u>ge</u>ous.

Write five sentences using words from the table above.

1. _____
2. _____
3. _____
4. _____
5. _____

Boost Spelling Skills 2

Suffixes

'-ous', '-ious' Words

creat<u>ive</u>

Read the passage and highlight the '**-ous**' and '**-ious**' words.

William Shakespeare wrote a famous play called *A Midsummer Night's Dream*. It involves two sets of lovers; Hermia and Lysander and Helena and Demetrius. In the play, it is obvious that Hermia and Lysander love each other, but Hermia's father wants her to marry Demetrius, who her best friend Helena loves. Hermia and Lysander are rebellious and run away to get married, but get lost in a mysterious wood where fairies live. They are closely followed by Demetrius and Helena, who the King of the Fairies, Oberon, overhears arguing. He tells his mischievous servant Puck to use a magical potion, while they are unsuspicious and fast asleep, which will make Demetrius fall in love with Helena, as she will be the first person he sees when he wakes up. Puck mistakes Lysander for Demetrius and sprinkles the potion into his eyes by mistake when he is asleep. When he wakes up Lysander sees Helena first and falls in love with her, forgetting all about his previous love, Hermia. Oberon is furious about the ridiculous muddle that Puck has created, and tells him to sort it out. Puck is able to reverse the spell and miraculously the story has a happy ending and true love is victorious.

Hermia and Lysander.
Painting by
John Simmons (1870).

Suffixes

'-ous', '-ious' Words (continued)

creat**ive**

Find and write down six words from the passage on page 34 that end in '-**ious**'.

1. _____ 4. _____
2. _____ 5. _____
3. _____ 6. _____

Can you split these words into syllables?

marvellous	mar/vell/ous
tremendous	
carnivorous	
victorious	
adventurous	
mountainous	

Match the word with its meaning.

carnivorous	somebody who is very polite
serious	extremely silly
mischievous	tasty and delicious
courteous	meat eating
ridiculous	being truthful, not joking
scrumptious	causing trouble in a playful way

Boost Spelling Skills 2

Suffixes

'-ous', '-ious' Words

creative

Choose the correct word from the box to complete the sentences.

| anxious | dangerous | famous | delicious | furious |
| enormous | infectious | carnivorous | poisonous | generous |

1. My mum's apple pie is _____ with custard.
2. Tom was _____ about his driving test.
3. It was _____ of the boy to share all of his sweets.
4. All the fans cheered the _____ popstar.
5. It is _____ to swim near a shark!
6. An elephant is an _____ land animal.
7. _____ animals like to eat only meat.
8. Chicken pox is a very _____ disease.
9. Dad was _____ that someone had dented his new car!
10. Don't get near that snake, it is _____ .

Complete the word sums.

Tip: Change 'our' to 'or' before adding '-ous'.

vigour + ous = _____

rigour + ous = _____

glamour + ous = _____

odour + ous = _____

splendour + ous = _____

humour + ous = _____

Suffixes

'-ly', '-ally' Words

creat<u>ive</u>

Can you read and spell these words?

Set A		Set B	
'-ly' words	'-ally' words	'-ly' words	'-ally' words
gladly	totally	eagerly	eventually
gently	equally	hastily	frantically
quickly	finally	patiently	historically
bravely	actually	definitely	dramatically
quietly	initially	fortunately	traditionally
angrily	casually	carelessly	accidentally
hungrily	usually	immediately	occasionally
frequently	basically	accurately	automatically
nervously	gradually	generously	energetically
unexpectedly	magically	desperately	exceptionally

Guidance:
Add **'-ly'** to an adjective to form an adverb, eg, <u>glad</u> + <u>'-ly'</u> = gladly

If the root/base word ends in a consonant + **'y'**, change **'y'** to **'i'** before adding **'-ly'** eg: <u>angry</u> + <u>'-ly'</u> = angrily

If root/base word ends in **'-ic'**, add **'-ally'** eg: <u>frantic</u> becomes frantically.

Choose five words from the table above and write sentences to show you understand their meaning.

1. _____
2. _____
3. _____
4. _____
5. _____

Suffixes

'-ly', '-ally' Words

Read and highlight the '-ly' and '-ally' words.

Harry Potter slipped on the cloak and unexpectedly became invisible! Strangely, this cloak had been in his family for several years, but Harry did not know this until it was given to him as a Christmas present one year, while he was at Hogwarts School of Magic. Automatically, the cloak was handed down to the eldest in each new generation of Potters. Naturally, Harry was delighted to receive this magical gift. It was created by a wizard called Ignotus Peverell, who fortunately escaped death by wearing it. Apparently invisibility cloaks are made using the hair of magical creatures called Demiguise who live in Far East China. Demiguise are almost extinct, so invisibility cloaks are exceptionally rare and valuable throughout the wizarding world. Harry quickly found out, when he walked into the restricted area of Hogwarts wearing the cloak, that the only person who could see him in the whole school was Professor Dumbledore. The reason Dumbledore was able to do this was because he was an extremely powerful wizard so he knew a spell which could work against the strong magic of the cloak.

Find and write down eight different words from the passage ending in '-ly' or '-ally'.

1. _____
2. _____
3. _____
4. _____
5. _____
6. _____
7. _____
8. _____

Boost Spelling Skills 2

©Brilliant Publications Limited

Suffixes

'-ly', '-ally' Words

creative

| Quietly | Bravely | Equally | Anxiously | Gently |
| Initially | Automatically | Luckily | Frequently | Magically |

Choose the correct word from the box above to complete the sentences.

1. _____ , the knight fought the fierce dragon.
2. _____ , we waited to see if everyone had been rescued.
3. _____ , Harry Potter put on the cloak and became invisible.
4. _____ , she tiptoed into the silent house.
5. _____ , my mobile phone reset the time to an hour later.
6. _____ , Uncle Tom divided the sweets between the boys.
7. _____ , has the same meaning as the word 'often'.
8. _____ , mum found the purse that she had lost.
9. _____ , the chef set all of the ingredients on the table.
10. _____ , the vet examined the dog's hurt leg.

Suffixes

'-ly', '-ally' Words

Match the word with the meaning.

hastily
frequently
initially
automatically

in a quick way
done without thought as a habit
many times
to begin with

Adding '**-ly**' to words to form adverbs.

Write the adverb for these adjectives.

bold	*boldly*	sad	
slow		rude	
loud		anxious	
quick		selfish	

Use one of the adverbs you have made to complete the sentences.

1. The tortoise slid _____ along the path.
2. We ran _____ inside out of the rain.
3. _____ I cannot come to your party.
4. The knight fought _____ in the battle.
5. Lucy _____ would not share any of her sweets.
6. He _____ did not say thank you for all my help.
7. The dog barked _____ when the postman came.
8. Mum waited _____ to hear if the operation was a success.

Suffixes

'-sure', '-ture' Words

creative

Can you read and spell these words?

'-sure' words		'-ture' words	
Set A	Set B	Set A	Set B
unsure	assure	future	moisture
ensure	reassure	capture	adventure
closure	leisure	picture	departure
insure	exposure	vulture	signature
pleasure	enclosure	mixture	miniature
measure	composure	creature	agriculture
cocksure	disclosure	puncture	temperature
treasure	displeasure	fracture	architecture
pressure	accupressure	furniture	manufacture

Guidance:
'-**sure**' used with words with /zur/ sound ending.
'-**ture**' often used with words with /chur/ sound ending.

Choose words from the table above and write sentences.

1. _____
2. _____
3. _____
4. _____
5. _____

Boost Spelling Skills 2

Suffixes

'-sure', '-ture' Words

creative

Read the poem and highlight the '-**sure**' and '-**ture**' words.

There was once a pirate called Captain Hook.
Whose villanous nature was his very signature.
His greatest enemy was the mischievous Peter Pan,
who liked to tease Hook for his own pleasure.

There was once a pirate called Captain Hook.
Who sailed in the 'Jolly Roger' to steal treasure.
Lurking near this ship was an enormous crocodile.
Who always caused him a lot of displeasure.

There was once a pirate called Captain Hook.
Who lost his left hand according to the literature.
In a sword fight with the impish Peter Pan,
it was eaten by the above-mentioned scaly creature.

There was once a pirate called Captain Hook.
Who felt a continual sense of pressure.
As he was stalked by that stout, greedy crocodile,
who had a hunger to eat the rest of him for good measure!

Boost Spelling Skills 2

Suffixes

'-sure', '-ture' Words

creative

| future | vulture | measure | creature | treasure |
| signature | puncture | temperature | pleasure | enclosure |

Choose the correct word from the box to complete the sentences.

1. Tigers are fierce wild _____s native to Asia.
2. The pirate had a wooden chest filled with _____ .
3. In the _____ man might travel to Mars.
4. Podma was ill in bed and had a high _____ .
5. The tyre needs replacing as it has a _____ .
6. The dog guided the sheep safely into the _____ .
7. Tom loves exercise and it gives him _____ to go to the gym.
8. He must sign his _____ on the back of the credit card.
9. The huge _____ circled around the dead animal.
10. Dad wants to _____ the length of the door.

Match the word with its meaning.

architecture	a break or crack in something
enclosure	art and design of buildings
leisure	a space that is closed in
miniature	spare time
fracture	very tiny

Boost Spelling Skills 2

Suffixes

'-tion', '-sion', '-cian' Words

creat<u>ive</u>

Can you read and spell these words?

'-tion'		'-sion'		'-cian'
Set A	Set B	Set A	Set B	
portion	protection	vision	decision	magician
question	exhibition	passion	explosion	optician
relation	promotion	invasion	compassion	dietician
solution	precaution	revision	impression	musician
pollution	ambition	illusion	discussion	electrician
intention	expedition	confusion	possession	beautician
infection	prescription	extension	transfusion	politician
direction	competition	television	permission	technician
reaction	reflection	occasion	comprehension	
collection	satisfaction	conclusion	supervision	

Guidance:
'-**tion**'   most common /shun/ sound
'-**sion**'   used mainly if root word ends in '**d/de**' or '**se**'
'-**cian**' used for people's jobs

Write sentences using five of the words from the table above.

1. _____
2. _____
3. _____
4. _____
5. _____

Suffixes

'-tion', '-sion', '-cian' Words

creat<u>ive</u>

Read the passage and highlight the '-**tion**', '-**sion**' and '-**cian**' words.

Alan Turing, who was born in 1912, was famous for being a very clever mathematician. His life has a fascination for people and he has been the subject of books, plays and films. A film about his life, called 'The Imitation Game' received eight Oscar nominations. Alan Turing had a passion for mathematics and gained a scholarship to Cambridge where he gained a distinction in his degree. He was called the father of the modern computer because he invented the idea of a machine that could decode and perform any set of instructions. He turned this revolutionary idea into a practical plan for a modern computer. During the Second World War, Alan made the decision to join the government code breaking department based at Bletchley Park in Buckinghamshire. He cracked the secret codes that Germany used for communication and so saved millions of lives. Alan Turing's contributions during the war were at first never publicly known about, because his work was classified as top secret. However Turing became a hero following the declassification of his work after the war, when all the secret files recognising his achievements were made public.

Find and write down eight different words from the passage that end in '-**sion**' or '-**tion**'.

1. _____
2. _____
3. _____
4. _____
5. _____
6. _____
7. _____
8. _____

Suffixes

'-tion', '-sion', '-cian' Words

creative

Choose the correct word from the table below to complete the sentences.

| television | competition | operation | prescription | revision |
| extension | optician | musician | invitation | transfusion |

1. Jack will collect the _____ from the chemist.

2. My uncle was poorly and needed a blood _____ .

3. I need to book an eye test with the _____ .

4. You need to do some _____ to prepare for the exam.

5. The _____ played the piano beautifully at the concert.

6. The whole class received an _____ to the party.

7. Dad is going to watch the football on the _____ tonight.

8. He was very excited to hear he had won the _____ .

9. Grandad is waiting to have an _____ to replace his hip.

10. The builders have now finished our kitchen _____ .

Suffixes

'-tion', '-sion', '-cian' Words

creative

Match the word with its meaning.

vacation
prescription
technician
discussion
compassion

a person doing practical work in a lab
a conversation
sympathy with others misfortune
holiday period
pills prescribed by the doctor

Write sentences using each of the words above.

1. _____

2. _____

3. _____

4. _____

5. _____

Boost Spelling Skills 2

Suffixes

'-ation Words

Can you read and spell these words?

'-ation' words		
location	invitation	alteration
donation	starvation	limitation
operation	admiration	adaptation
decoration	reservation	temptation
population	imagination	adaptation
celebration	condensation	resignation
irritation	conversation	consultation
punctuation	preparation	confirmation
illustration	conservation	transformation
demonstration	organisation	recommendation

Guidance

The suffix **'-ation'** is used to create nouns.

For most verbs **'-ation'** is just added to the root word, for example:
alter – alteration; confirm – confirmation.

If the root word ends in **'e'** remove the **'e'** before adding **'-ation'**.
For example, locate – location, invite – invitation.

Write four sentences using words from the table above.

1. _____
2. _____
3. _____
4. _____

Suffixes

'-ation' Words

creat*ive*

Choose the correct word from the box below to complete the sentences.

| operation | irritation | temptation |
| invitation | punctuation | illustration |

1. Poppy had an _____ to her friend's party.
2. All the _____s. in the book were beautiful.
3. Dad went into hospital for an _____ on his knee.
4. The constant noise caused a lot of _____
5. It was a big _____ to eat one of the delicious buns.
6. You need to put a _____ mark in that sentence.

The suffix '**-ation**' is added to a verb to make a noun.

> If the root word ends in '**-ate**' remove '<u>-ate</u>' and add '**-ation**'.
> If the root word ends in '**e**' remove the '<u>e</u>' and add '**-ation**'.
> OTHERWISE just add '**-ation**' but be aware there are some exceptions.

Fill in the missing words correctly.

Root word (verb)	Add the prefix '-ation' (noun)	Root word (verb)	Add the prefix '-ation' (noun)
imagine		donate	
decorate		transform	
alter		hesitate	
reserve		organise	
frustrate		confirm	
transport		demonstrate	

Boost Spelling Skills 2

©Brilliant Publications Limited

Suffixes

Syllable Splitting Rules

Syllable breakdown exercises can really help with spelling and reading skills and encourage pupils not to contract words. When a longer word is split into syllables, it is broken down into smaller spoken chunks for example: *hip/po/pot/am/us*. Each chunk is called a syllable. Remember each syllable has a vowel (**a, e, i, o, u**) in it, or a part time vowel (**y**). Say the word out loud and listen to the different beats or chunks of the word.

Note the syllable splitting guidelines and then ask pupils to complete the syllable exercises.

Focus on identifying the short and long vowel sounds. Closed syllables have a consonant, vowel, consonant (CVC) pattern and the vowel is <u>short</u> saying its <u>sound</u>, for example: <u>rob</u>/in, <u>mag</u>/net. Open syllables end in a <u>long</u> vowel and the vowel says its <u>name</u>, for example: <u>mu</u>/sic <u>pa</u>/per. Recognition of the specific vowel sound will also help pupils apply the rules for consonant doubling. (See double letter rule in the *Suffix Spelling Rules* section, pages 53 and 54.)

Syllable splitting guidelines

1. <u>Closed syllable</u>: Short vowel sound + consonant (consonant, vowel, consonant).
   Split after consonant – eg: rob/in, mel/on.

2. <u>Open syllable</u>: This syllable ends in a long vowel sound (consonant, vowel).
   Split after vowel – eg: wi/ser, ta/ble, su/per.

3. <u>Short vowel sound + 2 consonants:</u> (vowel, consonant/consonant, vowel)
   Split between consonants – eg: win/ner, stop/per.

4. <u>Compound word syllable:</u>
   Split between compound word – eg: green/house, rain/bow.

5. <u>Consonant + 'le' syllable</u>
   Usually split one letter before 'le' – eg: grum/ble, ma/ple.

6. <u>'r' combination</u>
   Split after <u>ur</u>, <u>ar</u>, <u>ir</u> – eg: c<u>ur</u>/tain, p<u>ar</u>/ty, c<u>ir</u>/cus.

Remember
- Split the prefixes and suffixes from the base word
  eg: un/**do**/ing, ex/**cite**/ment, re/**port**/er.
- Each syllable has a vowel or part-time vowel '**y**' in it.

Boost Spelling Skills 2

Suffixes

Syllable Splits

creative

Tip: Listen for long sounding syllable as in fa / mous.

Can you split the following words into syllables?

1.	glamorous	glam/or/ous
2.	pavement	
3.	wonderful	
4.	furniture	
5.	electronic	
6.	respectful	
7.	unlikely	
8.	epidemic	
9.	unfairness	
10.	tremendous	
11.	manufacture	
12.	optimistic	
13.	nervously	
14.	agriculture	

Suffixes

Syllable Splits

15.	wonderment	
16.	introduction	
17.	architecture	
18.	informative	
19.	determination	
20.	wastefulness	
21.	investigation	
22.	dangerously	
23.	mountainous	
24.	carnivorous	
25.	departure	
26.	unexpextedly	
27.	judgemental	
28.	argumentative	
29.	reinforcement	
30.	contamination	

Dictation Exercises

Suffixes

Note: Target words are underlined.
Keywords are in *italics*.
Harder dictation exercises in **bold**.

'-ic' word endings

1. *Perhaps* we could have a picnic?
2. We were stuck in a traffic jam for a long time.
3. Molly was sad when she *heard* the tragic story.
4. The bad news spread like an epidemic.
5. **The king thinks that the knight was very heroic.**
6. **I could see my sister was allergic to bee stings.**
7. This piece of music is *difficult* to play.
8. **There was a panic when the *experiment* went wrong.**

'-ive' word endings

1. My relative, has just got a new car.
2. I am positive that the earth is round!
3. That ruby ring will be too expensive.
4. The artist was creative with his painting.
5. **Do you think a lemon is a massive *fruit*?**
6. Another name for an adjective is a describing word.
7. **The aggressive dog barked loudly at the little cat.**
8. **The detective was *busy* looking for clues.**

'-ous' word endings

1. All the fans waved at the famous popstar.
2. The boy was nervous about the exam he had to take.
3. A *woman* saw an enormous fish floating in the sea.
4. All the carnivorous animal wanted was the red meat!
5. **The ship Titanic sank on its disastrous maiden voyage.**
6. It took a tremendous effort to *plant* all the trees.
7. **The poisonous snake had to be placed in a *separate* cage.**
8. **The *guard* was very courageous to stop the armed man.**

Boost Spelling Skills 2

Dictation Exercises

Suffixes

Note: Target words are underlined.
Keywords are in *italics*.
Harder dictation exercises in **bold**.

'-ious' word endings

1. The precious stone gleams in the sunlight.
2. Ben was envious of his friend's new sports car.
3. The new house had a very spacious back garden.
4. Jack was furious that his bike had been stolen.
5. **Chicken pox is most infectious before the rash *appears*.**
6. **The old man felt anxious as he couldn't remember his *address*.**
7. **We all *thought* Dad's stew tasted delicious.**
8. **The robber was notorious for stealing *bicycles*.**
9. **He was cautious walking on the icy pavement.**

'-ly' word endings

1. Quickly, the dog ran after the cat next door.
2. Bravely, the knight went into battle.
3. Unexpectedly, we were all locked out of the house.
4. Energetically, the boy ran around the track.
5. **Did you know that actually the *Earth* is not round?**
6. **"I can divide twenty equally by two," said Tom.**
7. **She was able to accurately *answer* the *question*.**
8. **Tom will definitely go swimming today, *although* not until later.**

'-sure' word endings

1. My *cousin* was unsure if he could come.
2. I like to do painting in my leisure time.
3. "Can you measure my *height*?" said Tom.
4. The closure of the pit upset the miners.
5. **The farmer put all of the pigs into a *separate* enclosure.**
6. **The *library* manager will reassure his staff that they won't lose their jobs.**
7. **The exposure to the cold gave the *guide* frostbite.**
8. **Can you *imagine* the fans' displeasure when the football club closed?**

Boost Spelling Skills 2

Dictation Exercises

Suffixes

Note: Target words are underlined.
Keywords are in *italics*.
Harder dictation exercises in **bold**.

'-ture' word endings
1. Dad fell off the ladder and has a fracture in his leg.
2. In the morning a vulture swoops down to the ground.
3. You must move all your furniture by the end of the day.
4. Please can you put a *quarter* of the mixture in that cake tin.
5. **The moisture of the dew made the grass sparkle in the sunlight.**
6. **It was a warm day but the temperature was not very high.**
7. "Write your signature on the dotted line," said the lawyer.
8. **My brother set off on an adventure sailing around the world.**

'-tion' word endings
1. Can I have a small portion of cheese?
2. My uncle will pick me up from the station.
3. Have the invitations to the party been posted?
4. The wind changed direction and it became colder.
5. **There was no accommodation at the inn for Mary.**
6. I could see a lot of paintings at the art exhibition.
7. **The doctor wrote me out a prescription to take to the chemist.**
8. *Frequently* Mum liked to enter a competition to win a car.

'-sion' word endings
1. The eye test showed she had good vision.
2. He knows it is *important* to do his revision.
3. Mum had a passion for growing lots of flowers.
4. "What is on the television tonight?" said Dad.
5. **Can we have a discussion about which holiday *location* is best?**
6. **Reading comprehension is not my *favourite* subject.**
7. **My *relation* had a blood transfusion when he was in hospital.**
8. "You need to have permission to attend this club," said the man.

'-cian' word endings
1. The magician produced a rabbit from the hat.
2. The mathematician knew the *answer* to the sum.
3. The electrician needed a *piece* of cable to finish the job.

©Brilliant Publications Limited

Boost Spelling Skills 2
55

slipped

Suffix Spelling Rules

Double Letter Rule

For most <u>one</u> syllable words ending in <u>one</u> short vowel and <u>one</u> single consonant, (the 1-1-1 rule) you need to **DOUBLE** the final consonant *to keep the vowel sound short* before adding a suffix that starts with a vowel: '**ed**', '**ing**', '**er**', '**est**' or '**y**'. For example:

    drag   dragged   dragging

    stop   stopped   stopping   stopper

Common exceptions are base/root words ending in '**w**' and '**x**'.

For example: *stew*: stews, stewed, stewing

                flex: flexes, flexing

y rule

* To add a suffix to a word that ends with '**y**', **change** the '**y**' to an '**i**' and add the suffix.

    For example: happy + ly   happily.

* Keep the '**y**' if adding '**-ing**', for example, hurry – hurrying.

* For words ending in a vowel plus '**y**', **KEEP** '**y**' and add the suffix.

annoy	annoyed	annoying
play	played	playing
spray	sprayed	spraying

e rule

* **DROP** the '**e**' before adding a vowel suffix '**-ing**', '**-ed**', '**-er**', '**-able**', or '**-ous**', for example:

| bake | baked | baker | bakable |
| move | moved | mover | movable |

* **KEEP** the '**e**' before adding a consonant suffix: '**-ful**', '**-less**', '**-ly**', '**-ment**',

    for example:

| hope | hopeful | hopeless |
| love | loveless | lovely |

* **KEEP** the '**e**' if words end in '**ce**' or '**ge**' before adding the suffix '**-able**' (to keep '**c**' or '**g**' soft), for example:

| replace | replaceable | dance | danceable |
| manage | manageable | encourage | encourageable |

Boost Spelling Skills 2

Suffix Spelling Rules

Double Letter Rule

slipped

For most <u>one</u> syllable words ending in <u>one</u> short vowel and <u>one</u> single consonant, (the 1-1-1 rule) you need to DOUBLE the final consonant to keep the vowel sound short before adding a vowel suffix: '-ed', '-ing', '-er', '-est' or '-y'.

For example: shop   sho**pp**ed   sho**pp**ing   sho**pp**er.

Complete the chart.

	Add '-ed'	Add '-ing'	Add '-er'
rub			
plan			
shop			
wrap			
stop			
dim			
knit			
drum			

Add '-er' or '-ing' to the word in brackets to complete the sentences below.

Tip: Don't forget to double!

1. We want to move to a _____ house. (big)
2. The little dog is _____ his tail. (wag)
3. Tom is in a _____ gala today. (swim)
4. He put the pencils and _____ in a tin. (rub)
5. Yasin is the _____ of the race. (win)
6. A policeman is _____ the traffic. (stop)

slipped

Suffix Spelling Rules

'e' Rule

Drop the final 'e' usually if adding a suffix starting with a vowel (**a, e, i, o, u**).
Drop the final 'e' to add part time vowel '**y**'.

Write the new words.

1. ice + y = _____
2. bone + y = _____
3. laze + y = _____
4. grease + y = _____
5. love + ing = _____
6. share + ed = _____
7. write + er = _____
8. decide + ing = _____
9. fame + ous = _____
10. nerve + ous = _____
11. excite + able = _____
12. believe + able = _____
13. accuse + ing = _____
14. decide + ing = _____
15. argue + able = _____

Suffix Spelling Rules

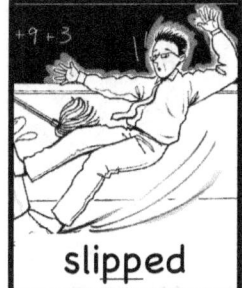
slipped

'e' Rule

KEEP the 'e' if adding a suffix starting with a consonant: '**-ful**', '**-less**', '**-ly**' or '**-ment**'.

For example: hop**e**ful, hop**e**less

Choose the correct word from the box below to complete the sentence.

| rudely | hopeful | excitement | useless | careful | bravely |

1. There was much _____ at the pop star's visit.
2. _____ the knight fought the fierce dragon.
3. The mobile phone was _____ without a charger.
4. He was _____ that he would get extra pocket money.
5. _____ Tom stamped his feet because he could not have any sweets.
6. You must be _____ when you cross the busy road.

KEEP the 'e' if words end in '**ce**' or '**ge**' before add suffix '**-able**'.

For example: servic**e** – servic**e**able

Finish these word sums.

1. manage + able = _____
2. notice + able = _____
3. knowledge + able = _____
4. change + able = _____

Boost Spelling Skills 2

©Brilliant Publications Limited

Suffix Spelling Rules

'y' Rule

slipped

CHANGE the 'y' to 'i' and add the suffix.
For example: spy, – spies

Complete the chart.

	Add '-es'	Add '-er'	Add '-ed'
tidy			
copy			
carry			
worry			
empty			
supply			

KEEP the 'y' if there is a vowel plus 'y', for example, enjoy enjoys.
KEEP the 'y' if adding '-ing', for example, hurry – hurrying.

Complete the word sums.

1. manage + able = _____
2. enjoy + ed = _____
3. buy + er = _____
4. play + ing = _____
5. obey + ed = _____
6. destroy + er = _____
7. marry + ing = _____
8. survey + ed = _____
9. employ + ment = _____

Boost Spelling Skills 2
©Brilliant Publications Limited

Suffix Spelling Rules

'y' Rule

slipped

Change or keep the 'y'?

Add '-**ed**' or '-**ing**' to the word in the bracket before writing it in the gap.

1. Poppy has a _____ egg and sausage for tea. (fry)

2. Have you _____ your bedroom yet? (tidy)

3. It was _____ that she missed the bus. (annoy)

4. The teacher _____ the picture on the wall. (display)

5. The dog is _____ a bone in the garden. (bury)

6. Six pegs _____ by two makes twelve pegs. (multiply)

7. _____ the rules is not a good idea. (disobey)

8. The water is _____ from the garden hose. (spray)

9. Poppy _____ to catch up with her friends. (hurry)

10. The young boy was _____ a red suitcase. (carry)

Dictation Exercises

Suffix Spelling Rules

Double letter rule
1. We are going <u>swimming</u> today.
2. Put the <u>stopper</u> on that bottle.
3. The little dog <u>wagged</u> his tail.
4. My brother is a <u>chatty</u> person.
5. She <u>rubbed</u> the sun cream on her face.
6. It was the <u>biggest</u> car she had ever seen.
7. The <u>drummer</u> marched down the street.
8. She <u>hugged</u> her friend to cheer her up.
9. Mum <u>slipped</u> on the ground and hurt her leg.
10. Have you <u>planned</u> to go <u>shopping</u> this week.

'e' rule (Drop the 'e')
1. Muhamed was loving his <u>shiny</u> new bike.
2. Are you <u>using</u> your new lawn mower.
3. The man could not have been any <u>ruder</u>.
4. The vet was <u>caring</u> for the sick dog.
5. We are <u>moving</u> in the summer holidays.

'e' rule (Keep the 'e')
1. The garden flowers had a <u>lovely</u> smell.
2. This gadget is <u>useless</u> because it does not work.
3. I know he will be punished for his <u>rudeness</u>.
4. Please be <u>careful</u> when you cross the road.
5. She made no <u>movement</u> to get out of bed.

y rule (Change 'y' to 'i')
1. The farmer <u>supplied</u> us with eggs.
2. I have <u>emptied</u> the waste paper bin.
3. He has <u>tidied</u> up all the rubbish.
4. How many <u>pennies</u> are in that tall jar?
5. Do you think you are <u>luckier</u> than me.

y rule (Keep the 'y')
1. My gran <u>enjoys</u> going to the beach.
2. She <u>played</u> with the dog in the garden.
3. I can't help <u>worrying</u> about the test.
4. Please do not lose those car <u>keys</u>.
5. The girl was <u>crying</u> because she lost her toys.

Functions of Suffixes

Making Comparatives: Adding Vowel Suffixes '-er' and '-est'

poppies

Standard		
old	older	oldest
fast	faster	fastest
dark	darker	darkest
long	longer	longest
rich	richer	richest
loud	louder	loudest

Short vowel + consonant		
big	bigger	biggest
fat	fatter	fattest
wet	wetter	wettest
hot	hotter	hottest
sad	sadder	saddest
thin	thinner	thinnest

Ending in 'e'		
nice	nicer	nicest
wide	wider	widest
fine	finer	finest
safe	safer	safest
late	later	latest
brave	braver	bravest

Consonant + 'y'		
dry	drier	driest
easy	easier	easiest
busy	busier	busiest
early	earlier	earliest
angry	angrier	angriest
happy	happier	happiest

Guidance

1 syllable words ending in **1 vowel + 1 consonant**	Double the consonant before adding '**-er**' or '**-est**'
Words ending in '**e**'	Drop the '**e**' before adding suffix '**-er**' or '**-est**'
Words ending in **consonant + 'y'**	Change '**y**' to '**i**' then add either '**-er**' or '**-est**'

Show me activity

Using the whiteboard ask pupils to write the comparatives from a target word remembering the guidance and then use the word in a sentence.

Teacher's Tips

Boost Spelling Skills 2

©Brilliant Publications Limited

Functions of Suffixes

Making Comparatives

poppies

> Adding vowel suffixes '-**er**' + '-**est**'
>
> The suffix '-**er**' can be added to adjectives to compare one noun to another.
>
> The suffix '-**est**' adds the meaning 'most' to adjectives.
>
> small – smaller – smallest

Fill in the missing words.

> **Tip:** If word ends in a short vowel and a consonant, double the last letter before adding the suffix.

	comparative + '-er'	superlative + '-est'
old		
big		
thin		
loud		
sharp		
cheap		

Add '-**er**' or '-**est**' to complete these word sums.

> **Tip:** Change 'y' to 'i' before adding the suffix.

busy + er = _____   ugly + est = _____

tiny + est = _____   juicy + er = _____

lazy + er = _____   happy + est = _____

Boost Spelling Skills 2

Functions of Suffixes

Making Comparatives

poppies

Complete the sentences by adding '-**er**' or '-**est**' to the word in brackets.

1. 1. Molly has to get up _____ than her sister. (early)

2. My new fur slippers are the _____ I have owned. (cosy)

3. Jack is busier than Tom but Dan is the _____ person. (busy)

4. This shirt is dirty but your shirt is even _____ . (dirty)

5. I feel _____ knowing that I do not have to sit an exam. (happy)

6. I thought I was lucky but you are even _____ than me. (lucky)

7. These strawberries are the _____ I've ever tasted. (juicy)

8. My suitcase is heavier than yours but that suitcase is the _____ one. (heavy)

Functions of Suffixes

Making Plurals: Adding '-s' or '-es'

poppies

Regular words just add '-s'	
chair	chairs
book	books
table	tables
house	houses
flower	flowers
pencil	pencils
animal	animals
computer	computers

f / fe 'f' changes to 'v' and add '-es'		EXCEPTIONS
calf	calves	roof – roofs
leaf	leaves	chief – chiefs
wolf	wolves	cliff – cliffs
scarf	scarves	
wife	wives	
knife	knives	
shelf	shelves	
thief	thieves	

'ch', 'sh', 'ss' and 'x' words: Add '-es'	
bench	benches
peach	peaches
witch	witches
bush	bushes
dish	dishes
class	classes
dress	dresses
box	boxes
fox	foxes

Common Irregular Words	
foot	feet
goose	geese
tooth	teeth
mouse	mice
child	children
person	people
woman	women
sheep	sheep
fish	fish
ox	oxen
person	people
cactus	cacti

Consonant plus 'y': 'y' changes to 'i' and add '-es'	
baby	babies
lorry	lorries
poppy	poppies
story	stories
berry	berries
puppy	puppies
family	families
country	countries

Vowel plus 'y': Keep 'y' and add '-s'	
toy	toys
tray	trays
turkey	turkeys
trolley	trolleys
valley	valleys
donkey	donkeys
cowboy	cowboys
monkey	monkeys

Boost Spelling Skills 2

Functions of Suffixes

Making Plurals 1

Many words just add '-s' to form the plural.
Add '-**es**' to words ending in 'ch', 'sh', 'ss', ' x'.

poppies

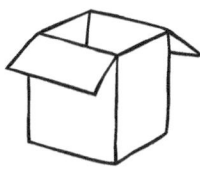 One box

 Three boxes

Add '**es**' to make these words plural.

1. wish _____
2. match _____
3. box _____
4. bush _____
5. glass _____
6. branch _____

7. coach _____
8. dress _____
9. peach _____
10. cross _____
11. marsh _____
12. fox _____

Write the plural of the words in the bracket.

1. There was a lot of noise in the _____ . (class)

2. "Can you put the _____ in the sink?" said Dad. (dish)

3. The man was painting the _____ in the park. (bench)

4. There were plenty of sandy _____ . (beach)

5. She put lots of _____ on the birthday card. (kiss)

6. The artist put the _____ in the paint pot. (brush)

Boost Spelling Skills 2

©Brilliant Publications Limited

67

poppies

Functions of Suffixes
Making Plurals 2

Many words add '-s' to form the plural.
Words ending in 'f' or 'fe' change f/fe to 'v' and then add '-es'.

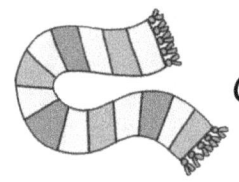 One scarf

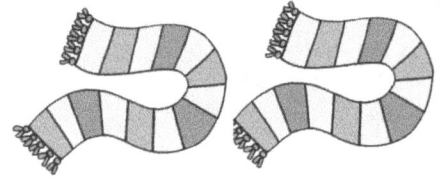 Two scarves

Make these words plural.

1. half _____
2. shelf _____
3. leaf _____
4. life _____
5. wife _____
6. calf _____
7. elf _____
8. knife _____
9. loaf _____
10. wolf _____
11. scarf _____
12. thief _____

Write the plural of the words in the bracket.

1. She baked some _____ of bread in the oven. (loaf)
2. Do two _____ make a whole? (half)
3. Some _____ stole the gold cups. (thief)
4. Be careful with those sharp _____ . (knife)
5. Mum is knitting some woollen _____ . (scarf)
6. Did King Henry VIII have six _____ ? (wife)

Functions of Suffixes

Making Plurals 3

poppies

Many words add '-s' to form the plural.
Words ending in 'y' change the 'y' to 'i' and then add '-es'.

 One puppy

 Two puppies

Make these words plural.

1. sky _____
2. city _____
3. pony _____
4. cherry _____
5. lorry _____

6. fly _____
7. baby _____
8. jelly _____
9. story _____
10. lady _____

Tip: Keep the 'y' and add '-s' if there is a vowel before it.

 One monkey

 Two monkeys

1. boy _____
2. valley _____
3. holiday _____
4. donkey _____

5. key _____
6. tray _____
7. toy _____
8. trolley _____

©Brilliant Publications Limited

Boost Spelling Skills 2
69

Functions of Suffixes

Making Plurals 4

Write the plural.

poppies

Tip: Remember the rules

1. bike _____
2. box _____
3. elf _____
4. penny _____
5. leaf _____
6. coach _____
7. tray _____
8. jelly _____
9. grass _____
10. beach _____
11. fox _____
12. life _____
13. monkey _____
14. party _____
15. dish _____
16. knife _____

Rewrite the whole sentence making everything plural.

1. The horse was in the field. *The <u>horses were</u> in the <u>fields</u>.*
2. There was a box on the carpet.
   _____
3. The baby was in the pram.
   _____
4. The monkey was at the zoo.
   _____
5. The lorry was on the road.
   _____
6. The knife was on the shelf.
   _____
7. The fairy was granting a wish.
   _____

Functions of Suffixes

Making Plurals 5

Rewrite these sentences putting the underlined words into the plural.

poppies

1. The <u>fox</u> will hunt in the night.
   _____

2. The cat and dog play in the <u>bush.</u>
   _____

3. Can you put the <u>peach</u> in the bowl?
   _____

4. I can see the <u>coach</u> coming down the road.
   _____

5. Jess took the party <u>dress</u> out of the wardrobe.
   _____

6. Jack put up the <u>shelf</u> in the bedroom.
   _____

7. I can see the little <u>calf</u> in the field.
   _____

8. The young <u>thief</u> stole the gold <u>ring</u>.
   _____

9. The <u>leaf</u> fall off the <u>tree</u> in the autumn.
   _____

10. Be careful of the sharp <u>knife</u>.
    _____

Boost Spelling Skills 2

Functions of Suffixes

Changing Tense: Adding '-ed' or '-ing'

popp**ies**

| asking | jumped | popped | baking | robbed |

Choose the correct word to fill in the gaps.

1. A red balloon _____ at the party yesterday.
2. The teacher is _____ us a question.
3. The little girl _____ over the puddle.
4. Jack is busy _____ a chocolate cake.
5. The other day a man _____ the local bank.

Adding '**-ed**' + '**-ing**' to words ending in '**e**'.

Tip: Remember to drop the '**e**' to add '**-ing**' or '**-ed**'.

1. dance + ed _____
2. live + ing _____
3. write + ing _____
4. bake + ed _____
5. escape + ed _____
6. hope + ing _____
7. close + ed _____
8. ignore + ing _____
9. arrive + ing _____
10. manage + ed _____

Functions of Suffixes

poppies

Changing Tense: Adding '-ed' or '-ing'

Adding '**-ed**' or '**-ing**' to words ending with a short vowel and a consonant.

Tip: Double the consonant before adding the suffix.

1. stop + ed _____
2. hop + ing _____
3. knit + ing _____
4. grab + ed _____
5. trip + ed _____
6. clap + ed _____

Complete the chart.

	Present tense + '-s'	Past tense + '-ed'	Present participle + '-ing'
walk	walk<u>s</u>	walk<u>ed</u>	walk<u>ing</u>
shout			
move			
wrap			
dance			

Functions of Suffixes

poppies

Changing Parts of Speech: Nouns into Adjectives

Match up the correct adjective with the noun.

Nouns		Adjectives
poison		woollen
pain		beautiful
ugly		painful
magnet		poisonous
wool		ugliness
beauty		magnetic

(poison → poisonous)

Add '-y' to change these nouns into adjectives.

Tip: Remember to drop the 'e' <u>before</u> you add the suffix '-y'.

Noun	Adjective	Noun	Adjective
mess	messy	itch	
ice		dirt	
sleep		juice	
shade		sand	

Select one of the adjectives from the table above to fill in the gaps.

1. I have to tidy up my _____ bedroom.

2. We sat in a _____ spot out of the sun.

3. The orange was very sweet and _____ .

4. Do not slip on the _____ path.

5. Poppy wanted to scratch the _____ spot.

Boost Spelling Skills 2

Functions of Suffixes

Changing Parts Of Speech: Verbs and Adjectives into Nouns

popp**ies**

Sort the following nouns into the correct boxes.

| darkness | station | enjoyment | illness | infection |
| payment | happiness | relation | treatment | |

'-tion' words	'-ment' words	'-ness' words

Add suffix '-**ness**' or '-**ment**' to change these verbs and adjectives into nouns.

to treat	treatment	kind	
to punish		fit	
to move		rude	
to amaze		quiet	

Add '-**tion**' or '-**ation**' to change these verbs into nouns.

Tip: Drop the 'e' before you add vowel suffix '-**ation**' if word ends in 'e'.

to admire	admiration	to operate	
to invent		to correct	
to inform		to attract	
to react		to prepare	

Boost Spelling Skills 2

Functions of Suffixes

Changing Parts Of Speech: Adjectives and Nouns into Verbs

poppies

Add suffix '-**en**' to change these adjectives and nouns into verbs.

soft		sharp	
wide		loose	
neat		short	
sweet		thick	
height		strength	

Select an '-**en**' word from the table above to complete the sentences below.

Tip: Find the word that is the opposite of the word underlined.

1. Dad will **widen** the <u>narrow</u> path.
2. Use the sugar to _____ the <u>sour</u> plums.
3. She will _____ the <u>long</u> dress today.
4. You must _____ the <u>tight</u> belt.
5. The <u>hard</u> butter will _____ in the heat.
6. _____ your <u>weak</u> tummy muscles at the gym.
7. Jack can _____ the <u>blunt</u> knife.
8. The cook will _____ up the <u>thin</u> gravy with corn flour.
9. You need to _____ up your <u>untidy</u> writing.
10. The shelf is too <u>low</u>, can you _____ it?

Boost Spelling Skills 2

Prefixes

Prefixes 'ex-', 'dis-' Words

superhero

The prefix '**ex-**' means *out of* or *utterly*.
The prefix '**dis-**' means *not*.

Can you read and spell these words?

'ex-' words	'dis-' words
exit	dislike
export	disagree
exile	discover
exhale	disaster
expand	disobey
exclude	disbelief
exterior	dishonest
explain	disgusting
extreme	disapprove
excavate	disinfectant
extinguish	disappearance
experiment	disappointment

Write sentences using words from the box above. You can use more than one word in each sentence if you wish.

1. _____
2. _____
3. _____
4. _____
5. _____
6. _____

Prefixes

Prefixes 'ex-' Words

superhero

Read the passage and highlight the words starting with prefix '**ex-**'.

Ella was a bit of a doll fanatic to say the least! When she heard there was an exhibition of Victorian dolls on Sunday at a gallery in the town, she was extremely eager to go and see it. She was excited because she had not got any Victorian dolls in her collection and thought it would be a good chance to expand it. Ella had expected her sister, Dana, to come with her, but she had excused herself at the last minute. However, Dana did have a good excuse for not going out because she needed to do a bit more revision for an English exam. Although Ella felt cross that her sister had changed her mind, she was still keen to go to the exhibition on her own.

On her arrival at the gallery, she examined all the exhibits and was surprised at how expensive some of the dolls were to buy. After she had explored the stalls at the exhibition, she went to the café in the gallery and had a cup of coffee and an excellent piece of chocolate cake. She had had an exceptionally good time but at exactly six o'clock Ella left the gallery and made her way home quite exhausted.

Find and write down as many different words from the passage starting with '**ex-**' as you can.

1. _____
2. _____
3. _____
4. _____
5. _____
6. _____
7. _____
8. _____
9. _____
10. _____
11. _____
12. _____

Prefixes

'dis-' Words

Read and highlight the words starting with prefix '**dis-**'.

superhero

It was a big disaster when Mrs Brown's precious diamond ring disappeared a few years ago. The ring was a family heirloom and had been in her family for years. It was also extremely expensive! Mrs Brown discovered it had gone missing when she returned home from a holiday and found her safe had been disturbed. She disliked the fact that she had to call the police about the theft. However, it caused her much more distress when she eventually found out who had taken her ring. There was much family discussion about the disappearance of the ring and it was discovered that her young niece Annie was to blame. Mrs Brown was upset that someone who she thought she knew well, was dishonest enough to steal from her. Happily, her niece did return the ring to her. Annie knew the whole family disapproved strongly of what she had done, and was really very sorry for all the trouble she had caused. Fortunately, Mrs Brown forgave her niece and Annie made up her mind that she would never be dishonest again.

Vocabulary

Heirloom: something valuable that has been in the family for a long time.

Find and write down as many different words from the passage starting with '**dis-**' as you can.

1. _____
2. _____
3. _____
4. _____
5. _____
6. _____
7. _____
8. _____
9. _____
10. _____
11. _____
12. _____

Boost Spelling Skills 2

Prefixes

'ex-', 'dis-' Words

superhero

| disappear | disappointed | disaster | disinfect | dishonest |
| excellent | expensive | experiment | export | explain |

Choose the correct word from the box to complete the sentences.

1. Floods, hurricanes and earthquakes are all natural _____s.

2. The magician made the white rabbit _____ !

3. She was _____ that her holiday was cancelled.

4. I need to _____ the toilet to get rid of germs.

5. The boy gained _____ marks in all of his exams.

6. The man was _____ because he stole from the shop.

7. I tried to think of the best way to _____ my feelings.

8. That bed is too _____ so we must get a cheaper one.

9. The scientist was completing his _____ in the laboratory.

10. An _____ is something that is sent to another country.

Prefixes

'ex-', 'dis-' Words

superhero

Draw lines to match the word with its meaning.

disintegrate		very tired
exhausted		refusing to obey
disobedient		infuriate, annoy
exasperate		no longer alive
disinfect		fall to bits
extinct		breathe out
disagree		to have a different opinion
exhale		to clense of germs

Make these words read the opposite by using the prefix '**dis-**' or '**un-**'.

1. happy _____unhappy_____
2. agree _____
3. lucky _____
4. appear _____
5. honest _____
6. wanted _____
7. well _____
8. true _____
9. grace _____
10. belief _____

©Brilliant Publications Limited

Boost Spelling Skills 2

Prefixes

superhero

'pro-', 're-' Words

The prefix '**pro-**' means *for* or *forward*.
The prefix '**re-**' means *again*.

Can you read and spell these words?

'pro-' words	're-' words
profit	reuse
project	return
provide	replace
protect	rebuild
produce	recover
promise	recycle
prohibit	recharge
prolonged	revision
propeller	rehearsal
professor	redecorate
protection	replacement
programme	rediscovered

Write sentences using words from the box above. You can use more than one word in each sentence if you wish.

1. _____
2. _____
3. _____
4. _____
5. _____
6. _____

Boost Spelling Skills 2

Prefixes

'pro-' Words

superhero

Read and highlight the words starting with prefix '**pro-**'.

Stephen Hawking is proclaimed as one of the greatest scientists that the world has ever seen. Working as a professor at Cambridge University, he proposed theories about how the world began. Unfortunately, he was just twenty one years old when he was struck with the onset of motor neurone disease, but the prospect of an early death acted as a spur for him to achieve as much as he could in the world of science. Eager for his theories to be widely known, he wrote a profusion of articles and books. His most famous book called 'A Brief History of Time' was probably the best-selling book of all time because it sold ten million copies! The book develops the readers' understanding of black holes, stars and the universe as a whole. Confined to a wheelchair as the disease took hold, Stephen Hawking's determination was an inspiration to many people, even when his body deteriorated and he lost his voice, he communicated by using a computerised one. After a long protracted illness, Stephen Hawking died in 2018 when he was seventy six years old.

Vocabulary

proclaimed: recognised
proposed: put forward
profusion: plenty, wealth of

Find and write down as many different '**pro-**' words from the passage as you can.

1. _____
2. _____
3. _____
4. _____
5. _____
6. _____

Prefixes

superhero

're-' Words

Read and highlight the words starting with prefix 're-'.

We must remember that recycling is important for our planet. If we do not reuse what we already have, we will end up running out of the world's natural resources. Most of the rubbish that we throw out can be reused, so it can be useful again. Recycled materials, such as paper, cardboard, plastic, glass and aerosol cans, can be reprocessed into new products. As a result the amount of rubbish sent to landfill sites is reduced. Glass is among several products that are 100% recyclable which means all the bottles and jam jars that are thrown away, can be melted down and used again and again. We should all think about reducing our rubbish and reusing items as it eases the burden on the environment and preserves natural resources for the future. For example, recycling paper saves trees and forests and also protects the rainforests which cannot be replaced.

Research shows that we are getting better at recycling in this country. However, everyone in Britain should make a bigger effort to increase the amount of our rubbish that we recycle as it is still only less than half of our rubbish that is in fact recyled.

Find and write down as many different 're-' words from the passage as you can.

1. _____
2. _____
3. _____
4. _____
5. _____
6. _____
7. _____
8. _____

Boost Spelling Skills 2

Prefixes

Prefixes: 'pro-', 're-' Words

superhero

recycle	repay	revision	recharge	recover
protect	propeller	programme	produce	profit

Choose the correct word from the box above to complete sentences.

1. Yasin will _____ all the money that he owes his mum.

2. We _____ paper, glass plastic and tins to help the environment.

3. The teacher told me I needed to do more _____ for the exams.

4. It is always better to make a _____ rather than a loss.

5. The boat's _____ churned up the water as it pulled away.

6. I hope Grandad will _____ soon after his long illness.

7. There is a television _____ tonight about the Second World War.

8. I wonder if the magician will _____ a rabbit out of his hat?

9. He will _____ the battery on his mobile phone.

10. This wet suit will _____ you from the cold sea water.

©Brilliant Publications Limited

Boost Spelling Skills 2
85

Prefixes

Prefixes: 'pro-', 're-' Words

superhero

Match the word with its meaning.

protracted
prohibit
reflection
rehearse

an image of something
to practise a performance
to ban or forbid something
in a long drawn out way

(protracted → in a long drawn out way)

Complete the words with the prefix '**re-**'.

re duce	_____ do	_____ pay
_____ fill	_____ cycle	_____ turn

Complete the words with the prefix '**pro**'.

pro tect	_____ fit	_____ vide
_____ test	_____ long	_____ ceed

Write sentences using four of the words from the boxes above.

1. _____
2. _____
3. _____
4. _____

Boost Spelling Skills 2

Prefixes

'pre-', 'sub-', 'super-', 'tele-' Words

superhero

Do you know these words?

'pre-' (before)	'sub-' (under, lower position)	'super-' (above)	'tele-' (over a distance)
predict	submarine	superstar	telescope
prevent	substandard	superman	television
precede	subzero	superior	telegram
preschool	submerge	supersede	televise
prehistoric	subway	supersonic	teleport
pretended	subtitle	supercharge	telephone
preservative	subtract	supermarket	telepathic
preparation	subside	supervisor	telegraph

Write sentences using six of the words from the table above.

1. _____
2. _____
3. _____
4. _____
5. _____
6. _____

Boost Spelling Skills 2
©Brilliant Publications Limited
87

Prefixes

superhero

'pre-', 'sub-', 'super-', 'tele-' Words

Read and highlight the words starting with prefix '**pre-**' '**sub-**' '**super-**' and '**tele-**'.

Harry Potts had a job as a supervisor during the day. He had to supervise a team of people who worked at a large supermarket in the town of Krypton. However he had another role that no one knew about because it was top secret. He was really a superhero who had superhuman magical powers! He was telepathic which meant he could read people's minds and knew what they were thinking. This was useful because he could prevent disasters from happening and save people from danger. With very little preparation he could teleport or move from one place to another at the speed of light.

The other day he knew that the crew on a submarine were in big trouble. The submarine's engine had failed and it had submerged to the bottom of the sea bed. There was no power and the temperature inside the ship had fallen to subzero. Harry Potts, otherwise known as Superman, flew to the rescue and got the engine to work. The happy crew were on the television yesterday praising the incredible superman who had saved their lives!

Write down words from the passage that start with the prefixes below

sub-	super-	tele-

Prefixes

'pre-', 'sub-', 'super-', 'tele-' Words

superhero

prescription	prehistoric	prevent	submarine	substandard
superstar	supermarket	subway	telephone	telescope

Choose the correct word from the box above to provide the answers.

1. A tunnel or underground passage. _____
2. A written note from the doctor to get medicine from a chemist. _____
3. In a time long ago: perhaps when the dinosaurs existed. _____
4. A shop selling more than just food. _____
5. An object used to allow you to talk to someone who's not with you. _____
6. Something you travel underwater in. _____
7. Someone who is very famous. _____
8. Something used to look at the stars more closely. _____
9. Something that is below normal quality. _____
10. To stop something from happening. _____

Prefixes

superhero

'pre-', 'sub-', 'super-', 'tele' Words

Write sentences using five of the words from the box below.

prescription	prehistoric	prevent	television	
televised	pretended	prepared	telephone	telescope

1. _____
2. _____
3. _____
4. _____
5. _____

Choose the correct word '**pre-**' or '**tele-**' word to complete the sentences.

1. Can you collect the _____ from the doctor?
2. She _____ the meal beforehand.
3. Dad watched the football game on the _____ .
4. Seatbelts can _____ injuries if you have a crash.
5. Dinosaurs were around in _____ times.
6. The man looked at the night sky with his _____ .
7. Gran _____ to be fast asleep but she was awake.
8. Can you ring me on the _____ tonight for a chat?
9. The TV programme was _____ around the world.

Complete the words using 'sub-' or 'super-'

_____ marine   _____ standard   _____ star

Boost Spelling Skills 2

Prefixes

Derivatives of the Prefix 'in-' (meaning not, in, on)

superhero

'in-' words				
intend	incredible	insane	inadequate	insecure
incapable	inactive	invisible	inhabit	incorrect

In most cases, the prefix '**in-**' changes the meaning of a word to the negative or opposite form, ie, visible and invisible, correct and incorrect.

This prefix changes when:

- words start with '**l**', then the 'in-' prefix becomes '**il-**'. For example, *legal* becomes illegal.
- a word starts with '**r**', then the 'in-' prefix becomes '**ir-**'. For example the negative meaning of *relevant* becomes irrelevant.
- a word starts with an '**m**' or '**p**' then the 'in-' prefix becomes '**im-**'. For example, *polite* becomes impolite and *mobile* becomes immobile.

il	im	ir
illegal	impress	irritate
illogical	impolite	irrelevant
illegible	immobile	irregular
illiterate	immortal	irrational
illustrate	impatient	irrespective
illusive	impossible	irresistible

Boost Spelling Skills 2

Prefixes

Derivatives of the Prefix 'in-' (meaning not, in, on)

superhero

illuminate	**im**migrate	**ir**replaceable
illegitimate	**im**personate	**ir**responsible

Put 'in-', 'il-', 'ir-' or 'im-' in the spaces to form the opposite meaning of the words.

_____polite	_____correct
_____responsible	_____legal
_____replaceable	_____visible
_____possible	_____legible
_____mobile	_____mortal
_____convenient	_____patient

Fill in the missing word using one of your answers from the box above.

1. Be careful with that vase, it is _____ .

2. Parking on double yellow lines is _____ .

3. Harry Potter became _____ when he put the cloak on.

4. It is _____ for me to reach that as I'm not tall enough.

5. Tomorrow is _____ as I am already doing something.

6. That statement is _____ . It should be the opposite!

Can you write two more sentences using two of the other words?

_____

_____

Prefixes

Derivatives of Prefix 'in-'

Match a word with its meaning. Use the dictionary if needed. How many can you match?

superhero

immortal	something that is against the law
immobile	to annoy somebody
illiterate	pretend to be somebody
illegal	cannot make up your mind
impersonate	not moving, stationary
irritate	someone that will live for ever
illogical	someone who is not able to read or write
indecisive	someone who has come to settle in a new country
immigrant	something that is hard to read
illegible	something not logical

Boost Spelling Skills 2

superhero

Prefixes

Prefix Syllable Splits

Split the following words into syllables.

Tip: Find the prefix first!

misjudge	mis / judge
revise	
dishonest	
exported	
reconstuct	
protesting	
discomfort	
submerge	
misbehave	
unfriendly	
explanation	
improvement	
proceeding	
mistrustful	
imperfection	
rechargeable	
unprotected	
inhabitant	
independent	

Boost Spelling Skills 2

Prefixes

Prefix Syllable Splits

superhero

uninterested	
disapproval	
extinguisher	
explanation	
reconstruction	
mismanagement	
understandably	
inconsiderate	
extraordinary	
superhuman	
relationship	
unemployment	
unimpressive	
responsibility	
disappearance	
transatlantic	
superintendant	
misfortune	
transportation	

Dictation Exercises

Prefixes

Note: Target words are underlined.

'ex-' words

1. You need to explain the problem.
2. She explored the island and found a large cave.
3. Meg was upset when she lost her expensive ring.
4. The chocolate cake you made tasted excellent.
5. I hope the experiment does not go wrong.

'dis-' words

1. The dishonest man stole ten pounds from the till.
2. The boy dislikes eating liver for his dinner.
3. There was a disgusting smell coming from the bin.
4. It was a disaster when the ship called Titanic sank.
5. I was excited when I discovered the parcel in my room.

'pro-' words

1. Those hens will produce lots of eggs this month.
2. Mum will provide lots of cakes for the picnic.
3. It is much better to have a profit rather than a loss.
4. The propeller on the plane had to be mended.
5. The umbrella gave me protection from the rain.

're-' words

1. I will never be able to repay your kindness to me.
2. "Can you reuse that plastic bag," asked Tom.
3. He will be returning from his holiday next Sunday.
4. I hope Sam will recover soon from his illness.
5. You will need to recharge the battery on the phone.

'pre-', 'sub-', 'super-' and 'tele-' words

1. She was prepared to prevent the dog jumping in the lake.
2. My little brother dropped his toy submarine in the subway.
3. The superstar attracted lots of crowds at the supermarket.
4. I think the telescope I got from the shop is substandard.
5. I did think that superman had some telepathic power.

Boost Spelling Skills 2

©Brilliant Publications Limited

Root Words

Root Words

Take off the prefix '**dis-**' or '**re-**' and write down the root word.

The root word is the basic word or part of a word with no prefix or suffix added.

chef

1. disappear = <u>appear</u>
2. reform _____
3. dislike _____
4. report _____
5. dishonest _____
6. refresh _____
7. disobey _____
8. return _____
9. disappoint _____
10. redecorate _____

Take away the suffixes and write down the root word.

1. Illness = <u>ill</u>
2. hopeless _____
3. truthful _____
4. amusement _____
5. national _____
6. quicker _____
7. sadness _____
8. friendly _____
9. gardening _____
10. poisonous _____

Choose the correct prefix below to add to the root word.

1. _____agree
2. _____happy
3. _____graph
4. _____behave
5. _____star
6. _____correct

| mis | auto | in | super | dis | un |

Boost Spelling Skills 2
97
©Brilliant Publications Limited

chef

Root Words

Sort the Root

Circle the root word.

> The root word is the basic word or part of a word with no prefix or suffix added.

remarkable	exporting
injected	disappointment
constructed	impressive
unkindness	infrequently
mistrustful	presentable

Sort the words into the chart below.

	Prefix	Root /base	Suffix
1.	re	mark	able
2.			
3.			
4.			
5.			
6.			
7.			
8			
9.			
10.			

Choose five words to make sentences.

1. _____
2. _____
3. _____
4. _____
5. _____

Boost Spelling Skills 2

Root Words

Word Origins

chef

A root word is a basic word with no prefix or suffix added to it (a prefix is a string of letters that go at the start of a word; a suffix is a string of letters that go at the end of a word). By adding prefixes and suffixes to a root word we can change its meaning. Most of the words in the English language are derived from Greek and Latin words.

/k/ spelt 'ch' (Greek in origin)

For example:
scheme, chorus, chemist, echo, character, ache, architect, chaotic, chaos, choir, chemistry, chorus, christening, Christmas

/sh/ spelt 'ch' (mostly French in origin)

For example:
chef, chalet, brochure, parachute, chandelier, champagne, Michelle, crèche, quiche, crochet, chateau, chauffeur

/g/ ending spelt 'gue'
/k/ ending spelt 'que' (mostly French in origin)

For example:
league, tongue, vague, rogue, fatigue, colleague, catalogue, antique, unique, cheque, mosque, grotesque, boutique, picturesque

/s/ spelt 'sc' (Latin in origin)

For example:
science, scene, discipline, fascinate, crescent, descend, ascend, scent, adolescent, adolescence

Root Words

chef

Root Word Origins: 'ch' saying /k/ or 'ch' saying /sh/

> The root word is the basic word or part of a word with no prefix or suffix added.

Can you read and spell these words?

'ch' saying /k/	'ch' saying /sh/
ache	chef
echo	chalet
choir	quiche
anchor	sachet
orchid	machine
stomach	machinery
monarch	brochure
chemistry	crochet
technology	avalanche
orchestra	parachute
character	moustache
Christmas	chandelier

Choose words from the box to make sentences.

1. _____
2. _____
3. _____
4. _____
5. _____
6. _____

Boost Spelling Skills 2

Root Words

Root Word Origins: 'ch' saying /k/ or 'ch' saying /sh/

chef

Read the passage and highlight 'ch' words sounding **/k/** in red and 'ch' words saying **/sh/** in blue.

Christopher Bell was head chef at a local primary school. He was busy making some quiches for the children to eat at lunchtime. He could hear the choir practising down the corridor. They were practising carols for the Christmas concert which was going to happen the following week. One of the children had such a high pitched voice that Christopher was certain that the small glass chandelier in the dining room would break! Suddenly he heard another loud noise. He knew that it was coming from the direction of the technology room. There was a small patch of lawn outside the technology room and a man was mowing the grass. The lawn mower had developed a mechanical fault and the machine was making an ear splitting grating noise. It was chaotic in the school that morning and all the noise was giving Christopher a bad headache. He was just thinking that he would have to pop out to the chemist to get some headache pills when all at once everything went quiet. Christopher breathed a sigh of relief and got on with making another mushroom quiche to have for lunch.

Find and write down different words from the passage that have:

'ch' saying /k/

1. _____ 5. _____
2. _____ 6. _____
3. _____ 7. _____
4. _____ 8. _____

'ch' saying /sh/

1. _____
2. _____
3. _____
4. _____

Root Words

chef

Root Word Origins:
'ch' saying /k/ or 'ch' saying /sh/

choir	anchor	chalet	headache	chemist
echo	chef	parachute	machine	

Choose the correct word from the box above to complete the sentences.

1. Tom shouted then waited for his _____ to come back.
2. She put the dirty clothes in the washing _____ .
3. The ship put down its _____ to stop it drifting.
4. The _____ at the hotel cooked some lovely meals.
5. He went to the _____ shop to collect the pills.
6. Tom stayed in a French _____ when he went skiing.
7. I had a bad _____ so I went to lie down upstairs.
8. A man wearing a _____ jumped out of the plane.
9. The school _____ sang carols at the concert.

Match the word with the meaning.

orchid		a small magazine containing information
brochure		a repeated sound
monarch		a large ornate light hanging from ceiling
echo		a showy flower
chandelier		a king, queen or emperor

Say the following words. Can you hear a 'ch' saying /k/ or 'ch' saying /sh/ sounds? Circle the correct sound.

Chef = /sh/ /k/	machine /sh/ /k/	Stomach /sh/ /k/
orchestra /sh/ /k/	chemistry /sh/ /k/	parachute /sh/ /k/

Boost Spelling Skills 2

Root Words

Root Origins Game

Match a word to its meaning. Cut out a set of cards for each child. Use the dictionary if needed. How many can you match?

chef

unique	a small shop selling fashionable clothes
mosque	a group of sports clubs
boutique	a mischievously playful person
rogue	the only one of a kind
league	a muslim place of worship

Boost Spelling Skills 2

©Brilliant Publications Limited

chef

Root Words

grotesque	a person somebody works with
picturesque	something old
colleague	tiredness or exhaustion
antique	very pretty
fatigue	ugly or strangely distorted

Homophones

Homophones

Homophones are words that sound the same but have different meanings. They also mainly have different spellings.

sun/son

ate	eight
bear	bare
berry	bury
blew	blue
brake	break
dear	deer
fair	fare

Boost Spelling Skills 2

Homophones

sun/son

flour	flower
for	four
grate	great
groan	grown
hair	hare
heal	heel
hear	here
hole	whole

Homophones

sun/son

hour	our
knew	new
knight	night
mail	male
main	mane
meat	meet
medal	meddle
pair	pear

Boost Spelling Skills 2

Homophones

sun/son

	peace	piece
	plain	plane
reign	rain	rein
	right	write
rowed	road	rode
	sail	sale
	saw	sore
	scene	seen

Homophones

sun/son

scent	sent
sea	see
stair	stare
tail	tale
their	there

they're

threw	through
throne	thrown

Boost Spelling Skills 2

Homophones

sun/son

to	too	two
waist	waste	
wait	weight	
way	weigh	
weak	week	
wear	where	
weather	whether	

Homophones

sun/son

Homophones are words that sound the same but have different meanings. They also mainly have different spellings too.

The word homophone originates from the Greek words *homo* (same) and *phon* (sound).

Underline the correct word.

1. Dad had to use the (break/brake) to stop the car.
2. The dog went to (bury/berry) the bone in the garden.
3. The postman delivered all of the (male/mail) that was in his sack.
4. Can you (hear/here) all that noise coming from the playground?
5. The (plain/plane) landed safely at the airport.

Write the correct homophone in the space.

peace or piece

"Can I have a _____ of pie?" said Tom.

Mum wants to have a bit of _____ and quiet.

meet or meat

There was a lot of _____ in the butcher's shop.

Poppy went to _____ her friends at the park.

weather or whether

I do not know _____ to come to the party.

The _____ was lovely as the sun shone all day.

Homophones

sun/son

Homophones are words that sound the same but have different meanings. They also mainly have different spellings too.

The word homophone originates from the Greek words *homo* (same) and *phon* (sound).

Write the correct homophone in the space.

plane or plain

The _____ flew across the Atlantic ocean to New York.

I need some _____ paper to print out my work.

medal or meddle

Jack won the race and was given a gold _____ .

"Please do not _____ in my business," said Adil.

sea or see

We always visit the _____ when we go on holiday.

Wow! Did you _____ that? It was incredible.

threw or through

Fred _____ the ball for his dog to retrieve.

The tunnel was very dark and it went right _____ the mountain.

Homophones

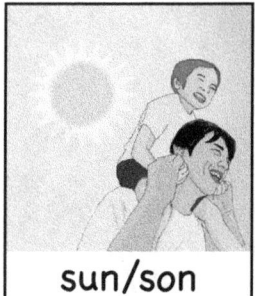
sun/son

'to', 'two', 'too'?

to	a word used to show movement
two	a number
too	- also, as well
	- extremely eg: too silly

Read the sentences and write '**to**', '**too**' or '**two**' in the spaces.

1. Adam went _____ the park at least twice a week.
2. The little white hen laid _____ eggs today.
3. Are we going _____ do some shopping for Grandad?
4. At the moment it is _____ wet to go out for a walk.
5. I am going _____ watch football on the television.
6. "_____ times four does not equal ten," said Tom.
7. Jack went _____ the garage to get his tool box.
8. Lola lives in Uxbridge and Jade lives there _____ .
9. You need _____ water the garden as the flowers are wilting.
10. I think there are _____ many cooks in the kitchen!
11. We waited for the traffic lights _____ change from red _____ green.
12. "Can we come with you _____ !" shouted the twins.
13. It is far _____ hot today _____ go for a run in the park.
14. You are likely _____ get burnt if you don't put sunscreen on.
15. Dad wants _____ buy _____ bags of compost at the garden centre.

©Brilliant Publications Limited

Boost Spelling Skills 2

Homophones

'there', 'their', 'they're'?

sun/son

there	'in that place', eg "Put the toys over *there*." There are … ; There is … ; There was … .
their	belonging to them, eg, *their* hats and coats.
they're	short form of *they are*, eg, *They're* lost!

Read the sentences and write '**there**', '**their**' or '**they're**' in the gaps.

1. _____ is no rain tomorrow so I can cut the grass.
2. _____ dog always barks at us.
3. _____ are lots of flowers in that garden.
4. I can see your spectacles over _____ .
5. Many trees lose _____ leaves by the winter time.
6. My grandparents told me that _____ going to Spain.
7. The children felt ill so the nurse took _____ temperature.
8. I can see some Easter eggs hidden by the chest over _____ .
9. _____ is a prize for the best homework!
10. _____ hoping to win the lottery tonight!
11. I did not know that _____ was any milk in the fridge.
12. They hoped that _____ project would win the prize.
13. _____ going on holiday for a month this year.
14. "Your table is over _____ by the window," said the waitress.
15. The children told me that _____ house was for sale.
16. Tom and Jack put _____ bikes in the shed over _____ .

Boost Spelling Skills 2

Homophones

Near Homophones

These words sound very similar but have different meanings and spellings. They are frequently confused, for example: *accept* and *except*.

sun/son

---

accept   means 'to take something that someone gives you'
For example:
Please accept my apology for being rude.

except   means 'something that is not included'
For example:
I like all sweets except chewy toffees.

Fill in the gaps in the sentence correctly using '**accept**' or '**except**'.

1. Please _____ this home-made cake as a thank you gift.

2. She has done all her homework _____ for maths.

3. My sister is going to _____ the university place she was offered.

4. Dad goes for a run every morning _____ for Sunday morning.

5. Cinderella was glad to _____ the invitation to the ball.

6. Can you all stay behind _____ for Tom?

7. Yasin will _____ the job if it is offered.

8. He plays football every day _____ Sunday

9. The charity shop will _____ your old toys

10. This gift is too expensive for us to _____ .

Homophones

sun/son

Near Homophones

These words sound very similar but have different meanings and spellings. They are frequently confused, for example: *affect* and *effect*.

---

affect (verb) means 'to change or make a difference to'
   For example:
   The cold weather affected my Grandad's bad leg.

effect (noun) means 'a result or consequence'
   For example:
   The effect of the snow was that the roads were slippery.

Fill in the gaps in the sentence correctly using '**affect**' or '**effect**'.

1. As an _____ of the rain, sports day was cancelled.
2. The Covid pandemic had an _____ on many people.
3. The hot weather will _____ what you wear.
4. Bad news can _____ people and make them sad.
5. The music had a good _____ and made him calm down.
6. Weight gain can be the _____ of over eating.
7. The train strike will _____ Tom's ability to get to work.
8. As an _____ of the storm a few trees have fallen down.
9. The children were all _____ ed by the sad story.
10. The loud music _____s her ability to study.

Boost Spelling Skills 2

Homophones

Sound Snap / Pairs

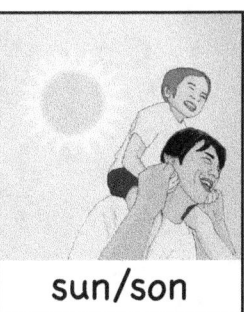
sun/son

Cut out the sets of cards and use them to play Snap or Pairs.

main mane	main mane
main	mane
meat meet	meat meet
meat	meet
brake break	brake break
brake	break
berry bury	berry bury
berry	bury

©Brilliant Publications Limited

Boost Spelling Skills 2
117

Homophones

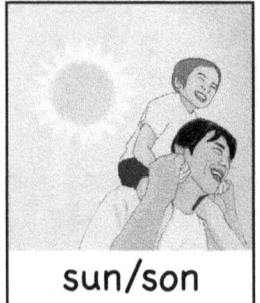
sun/son

mail male	mail male
mail	male
not knot	not knot
not	knot
plain plane	plain plane
plain	plane
which witch	which witch
which	witch

Boost Spelling Skills 2

©Brilliant Publications Limited

Homophones

sun/son

mist missed	mist missed
mist	missed
grate great	grate great
grate	great
right write	right write
right	write
knight night	knight night
knight	night

Homophones

sun/son

blew blue	blew blue
blew	**blue**
son sun	son sun
son	**sun**
medal meddle	medal meddle
medal	**meddle**
waist waste	waist waste
waist	**waste**

Dictation Exercises

Homophones

Note: Target words are underlined.

'two', 'to' or 'too'

1. I like <u>to</u> read a book a week.
2. There are <u>two</u> red cars on the drive.
3. Can I come <u>to</u> the shops <u>too</u>?
4. That comic will cost <u>two</u> pounds.
5. These sums are <u>too</u> easy for me <u>to</u> do.
6. Would you <u>two</u> girls like <u>to</u> come <u>too</u>?

'there', 'their' or 'they're'

1. <u>Their</u> house is bigger than my house.
2. <u>They're</u> all going out into the garden for a BBQ.
3. Stand <u>there</u> and wait for me please.
4. The trees are losing <u>their</u> leaves.
5. The boat over <u>there</u> is <u>their</u> boat.
6. <u>They're</u> all outside waiting for you with <u>their</u> bikes.

Homophones

1. Jill wore a <u>plain</u> red dress to the party.
   The <u>plane</u> landed on the runway.
2. Do not <u>break</u> that glass vase.
   Put the hand <u>brake</u> on the car.
3. Beef and pork are red <u>meat</u>.
   Kevin will <u>meet</u> us at 10 o'clock.
4. There was <u>peace</u> when the noise stopped.
   A <u>piece</u> of cake would be nice.
5. The <u>weather</u> forecast today is rain.
   It depends <u>whether</u> I can ride my bike.
6. She could not <u>hear</u> as she was deaf.
   Come <u>here</u> now or I will be cross.
7. My brother is a <u>male</u> child.
   The letter will go by air<u>mail</u> to America.
8. We like to <u>bury</u> our feet in the sand.
   I like to eat black<u>berry</u> pie.

Teacher's Tips (repeated in margin)

©Brilliant Publications Limited

Boost Spelling Skills 2
121

Silent Letters

Silent Letters

i_sland / pa_lm

Silent letters are letters that cannot be heard when the word is pronounced. More than half of the letters in our alphabet are silent in some words.

Read and highlight the words containing silent letters.

Everyone knows that Susie Lamb, the college cook, is a hard worker. One autumn evening she makes some shortbread biscuits and washes several sticks of rhubarb. She then kneads some pastry because she wants to make a lot of rhubarb pies. All of a sudden Susie hears such a lovely sound echoing all around the building; someone is playing a guitar really well. Susie often listens to music and the rhythm of the guitar makes her want to dance. She is a good dancer having had ballet lessons when she was younger. Susie wriggles her hips in time to the beat and starts to dance around the room. A banana skin which was left on the floor causes her to slip and fall down. She knows something is wrong when she feels a sharp pain in her knee before it goes numb. After a short while her knee feels a bit better so she stands up slowly and makes herself a cup of tea. However, Susie Lamb is in no doubt that her knee will feel much better very shortly. So she reminds herself to pick up the rogue banana skin before anyone else slips on it.

Can you find the words with silent letters in the passage?

4 silent **u** words				
4 silent **h** words				
3 silent **b** words				
3 silent **k** words				
2 silent **w** words				
2 silent **t** words				
1 silent **n** word				

Boost Spelling Skills 2

Silent Letters

Silent Letters

island / palm

Silent letters are letters that cannot be heard when the word is pronounced. More than half of the letters in our alphabet are silent in some words.

Read the words below and circle the silent letters.

lamb	castle	knock	scent
knife	wrong	plumber	knee
often	answer	scene	listen
wrist	comb	scissors	knitting
sword	fasten	crumb	science

Sort the words above into the correct boxes.

Silent **b**	Silent **c**	Silent **w**	Silent **t**	Silent **k**

Choose five of these words to make sentences.

1. _____
2. _____
3. _____
4. _____
5. _____

Silent Letters

island / pa_lm

Silent Letters: Card Game

2–4 players

1. Photocopy onto thin card and cut out the *silent letter* squares.
2. Shuffle cards and deal seven cards to each player and put the rest in a pile. Pick up the top card and put it face downwards by the main pile to start a discard pile.
3. Each player in turn picks the top card from the main pile (or he can pick up the last card the previous player discarded) and throws away a card.
4. The winner is the person who has collected the most families (in sets of 3) at the end of the game.

Silent b	Silent b	Silent b
lamb	comb	climb
Silent b	Silent b	Silent b
doubt	thumb	plmber
Silent w	Silent w	Silent w
wrist	write	wrong

Boost Spelling Skills 2
124   ©Brilliant Publications Limited

Silent Letters

Silent Letters: Card Game

island / palm

Silent w	Silent w	Silent w
wriggle	sword	answer
Silent h	Silent h	Silent h
hour	honest	school
Silent h	Silent h	Silent h
rhythm	while	when
Silent t	Silent t	Silent t
listen	castle	moisten

Silent Letters

Silent Letters: Card Game

i_sland / pa_lm

Silent t Chris**t**mas	Silent t this**t**le	Silent u g**u**ess
Silent u g**u**ide	Silent u g**u**ard	Silent u bisc**u**it
Silent u b**u**ild	Silent u g**u**itar	Silent c s**c**issors
Silent c s**c**ent	Silent c s**c**ene	Silent c des**c**end

Boost Spelling Skills 2

©Brilliant Publications Limited

Silent Letters

Silent Letters: Card Game

island / palm

Silent c	Silent c	Silent k
muscle	science	knight
Silent k	Silent k	Silent k
knead	knowledge	knitting
Silent k	Silent k	
knock	knife	

Boost Spelling Skills 2

Dictation Exercises
Silent Letters

Note: Target words are underlined.

Silent k
1. Granny was busy knitting a red jumper.
2. The Red Knight will not fight at night time.
3. Please put the knife and fork on the table.
4. All of a sudden there was a knock at the door.

Silent b
1. That little lamb was born yesterday.
2. A robin pecked at the crumb of bread.
3. The plumber will mend the tap in the bathroom.
4. There is no doubt that it will rain today.

Silent c
1. The hound follows the scent of the fox.
2. A policeman was at the crime scene.
3. The science teacher took the class into the lab.
4. Pass me the scissors so I can cut the string.

Silent t
1. Who lives in the castle on the hill?
2. Listen to the sound of the birds singing.
3. I often go for a swim in the mornings.
4. Can you fasten your seat belt please.

Silent w
1. He hurt his wrist when he fell down.
2. The knight picked up his sword.
3. I could not see what was wrong.
4. What is the answer to that question?

Boost Spelling Skills 2

©Brilliant Publications Limited

GLOSSARY

Analogy
Spelling by *analogy* is using the sound pattern of one word to make a prediction about the spelling pattern of a similar sounding word. In other words, using known words to spell unfamiliar ones.

For example: **could should would**

Adjective
An *adjective* is a word that describes and gives more information about a noun.

For example: a clever pupil, the shimmering sea.

Base words and Root words
A *base word* is the stand alone basic word that can also form other words when a prefix or a suffix is added.

For example: **'pack'** is the base word of: packet, package, unpack, repacked

A *root word* is a word or part of a word that can form a meaningful word when a prefix or suffix is added. It has its origins in an old Greek or Latin word.

For example: **'struct'** coming from the latin 'to build' is the root word of construct, destruct, instruct, destruction, etc.

Compound words
Compound words are made when two words are joined together to form a new word. The two words make sense on their own and the new word makes sense as well.

For example: 'toothpaste' and 'heavyweight'.

Homophones
Homophones are two or more words that sound the same but have different meanings and usually have different spellings.

For example:- rain (liquid water)
              reign (rule as a monarch)
              rein (horse lead)

Mnemonic
A *mnemonic* uses a pattern of letters, ideas, or associations to help jog the memory and remember a difficult word to spell.

For example: There is 'a rat' in separate.

GLOSSARY continued

Multisensory approach
This is the simultaneous use of visual, auditory, and kinaesthetic-tactile prompts which research shows enhances memory and learning.
For example: Use of *'Look, Say, Cover, Write, Check'* spelling sheets.

Noun
A *noun* is a word that names a thing such as an object, animal, place, person or feeling
For example: shoe, dog, lake, child, sadness

Prefix
A *prefix* is a group of letters placed before the root of a word which alter the meaning of the word. They are not words in their own right and cannot stand on their own.
For example: redo, misunderstand, export, autobiography

Suffix
A *suffix* is a set of letters that go at the end of a root (base) word, changing the meaning of the word. Some suffixes include: *'-ary'*, *'-able'*, *'-ance'*, *'-ate'*, *'-en'*, *'-ed'*, *'-ful'*, *'-ify'*, *'-ly'*, *'-ous'*. Suffixes can change parts of speech. For example, adding the suffix *'-ify'* changes the noun 'terror' into the verb *'terrify'*.

Syllable
A *syllable* is a beat of sound in a word.
For example 'gracefully' has three beats (**grace–/ful/ly**) but 'ghost' has only one syllable (**ghost**). Each syllable contains at least one vowel or part time vowel **'y'**.

Verb
A *verb* is a doing word in a sentence to show physical or mental action and it can also show a state of being.
For example: Mary raced downstairs. The old lady was upset

Unstressed vowels
Unstressed vowels are vowel sounds (*a, e, i, o* or *u*) that are difficult to hear when a word is said out loud. An example of a word with unstressed vowel sounds is 'interest'. When we say interest, it sounds more like 'intrest'.

Appendix

Irregular Verbs Past Tense

Most verbs form the past tense by adding '**-ed**'. Some verbs do not follow this regular pattern and these verbs are called *irregular* verbs.

Examples of some irregular verbs.

are / were
blow / blew
build / built
buy / bought
catch / caught
choose / chose
come / came
dig / dug
drink / drank
drive / drove
eat / ate
fall / fell
feed / fed
find / found
fly / flew
get / got
give / gave
go / went
hang / hung
have / had
hear / heard
hide / hid
hold / held
is / was
keep / kept

know / knew
leave / left
lends / lent
lose / lost
make / made
meet / met
put / put
read / read
ring / rang
run / ran
see / saw
sell / sold
send / sent
sing / sang
sit / sat
sleep / slept
speak / spoke
spend / spent
steal / stole
swim / swam
teach / taught
think / thought
wake / woke
win / won
write / wrote

Photo/Illustration Credits

Girl and dog; Clker Free Vector Images: Pixabay
Happy; Clker Free Vector Images: Pixabay
Hippo; Venita Oberholster: Pixabay
Paintbrush; Open Clipart Vectors: Pixabay
Newspaper; Gerd Altmann: Pixabay
Weight; Open Clipart Vectors: Pixabay
Cherry pie; Clker Free Vector Images: Pixabay
Hermia and Lysander painting by John Simmons (1870): Wikipedia
'Sorting hat'; Natasia Day: Pixabay
Crocodile; Dmitry Obramov: Pixabay
Dog; Eduardo RS: Pixabay
Doll: Janice Brown: Pixabay
Amethyst ring; Sara Graves: Pixabay
Stephen Hawking: Wikimedia Commons
Recycling box; Clker Free Vector Images: Pixabay

Page-top images:
Spelling Strategies – Hippopotamus; Dmitry Abramov: Pixabay
Keywords – Teacher and pupil; Brilliant Publications Ltd
Suffixes – Hand prints; No Longer Here: Pixabay
Suffix Spelling Rules – Slipped; Brilliant Publications Ltd
Functions of Suffixes – Poppies; Poppy field; Absolutely Free Photos
Prefixes – Superhero; Cosplay Images: Pixabay
Root Words – Pizza Chef; Christian Dorn: Pixabay
Homophones: Sun/son (merged) – Sun; Sabine Kroschie: Pixabay and
　　　　　　　　Father and son; Tilixia: Pixabay
Silent Letters – Beach; Rani Suarni: Pixabay

www.ingramcontent.com/pod-product-compliance
Lightning Source LLC
Chambersburg PA
CBHW081003180426
43192CB00042B/2435